RC
464
.K34
E38
1981

Edwards, Henry.

What happened to my
mother

DATE			

MAR 5 - 1982

BUSINESS/SCIENCE/TECHNOLOGY DIVISION

© THE BAKER & TAYLOR CO

What Happened to My Mother

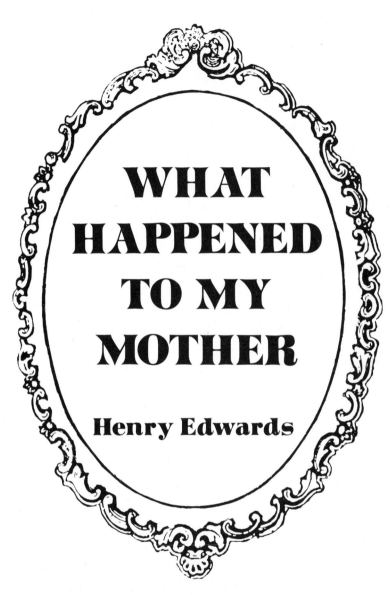

WHAT HAPPENED TO MY MOTHER

Henry Edwards

HARPER & ROW, PUBLISHERS, New York
Cambridge, Philadelphia, San Francisco,
London, Mexico City, São Paulo, Sydney

1817

The quotations on pages 131–132 are from *Mind Games* by Robert Masters and Jean Houston; those on page 140 are from *Awareness Through Movement* by Moshe Feldenkrais.

FIRST EDITION

Designer: Ruth Bornschlegel

Library of Congress Cataloging in Publication Data

Edwards, Henry.
  What happened to my mother.

  1. Katz, Esther Rebecca, 1914–   . 2. Mental
illness—United States—Biography. I. Title.
RC464.K34E38 1981   362.2'092'4 [B]   80–8684
ISBN 0–06–011088–0   AACR2

---

81 82 83 84 10 9 8 7 6 5 4 3 2 1

What Happened to My Mother is basically a true story. However, with the exception of the names of my parents and the people connected with the production of the motion picture *Sgt. Pepper's Lonely Hearts Club Band,* the names of individuals and institutions are fictitious. In addition, individual characteristics and locales have been changed.

H.E.

For my parents

What Happened to My Mother

1. My mother's mental illness came as a shocking, terrifying surprise.

It was the summer of 1976 and I was feeling euphoric: producer Robert Stigwood had asked me to write the motion picture version of *Sgt. Pepper's Lonely Hearts Club Band.*

Stigwood lived in Bermuda and I was invited to spend long weekends working at Palm Grove, his twenty-five-acre home base.

I had a luxurious five-room, two-story building all to myself, on an elegantly landscaped estate that housed an aviary where one hundred gaily colored parrots screamed their heads off day and night. Whenever I needed a break I could stroll through the gardens or talk to the birds. There was only one condition: that I be poolside at eleven each morning.

At that time I would be joined by the ruddy-faced Australian-born producer. He would be served his usual breakfast—a soft-boiled egg, black coffee, and a bottle of Perrier. He would read the newspapers and take the sun. We would discuss the news, trading opinions back and forth. By then he would be awake and ready to turn his attention to *Sgt. Pepper.*

I had set the film in "Heartland," an update of those idealized towns that were the backbone of the MGM Andy Hardy films. In Heartland, the water was always pure, the air always clean, and everybody brimmed with good cheer.

We would discuss the plot, act out some of the scenes, and throw suggestions back and forth. Periodically we'd jump into the pool to refresh ourselves.

"Hi, cuties." Robert's secretary, Joy McMillan, a redheaded, freckle-faced beauty, stood poolside. "Your father is on the phone," she told me. "He says it's urgent."

Sam never called me long-distance.

I climbed out of the pool and hurried across the lawn. In the study, I pushed down the blinking button and picked up the receiver. "Hi," I said. "It's Henry."

"Your mother thinks you're dead. Quick. Talk to her. Tell her you're all right."

"Hello," Esther said tentatively.

"It's Henry," I said, thoroughly confused about what was going on. "I'm fine."

"Is this you?"

"It's me!"

"It's not!" Esther slammed the phone down. I quickly dialed my parents' number in Brooklyn.

"Hello," said Esther.

"It's Henry!" Once again my mother slammed down the receiver.

Now I was beginning to feel frightened. I dialed again. This time I got Sam.

"Don't talk to him," I could hear Esther shouting.

"I can't talk to you." Sam hung up.

I kept trying them for hours. The phone would ring and no one would answer, or Esther would pick it up and hang up without saying a word. It took until evening before Sam and I could talk without interruption. "She's dozing, thank God," he said. Then he told me what had happened.

It had begun the day before when they were shopping.

Suddenly Esther had jumped off the curb and begun to run. "I'm being chased by a sound truck," she had screamed. "Can't you hear them? They're calling my name."

Sam looked around. There was no sound truck. No one was calling Esther's name.

"She had a total mental breakdown," Sam told me. "Last night when I was asleep, she got up, got dressed, and went outside. I found her running through the streets begging strangers for help. I've spent the whole day trying to keep her inside. Every time I turn my back she tries to get away."

"Why don't you take her to a doctor?"

"I tried that," he replied, "but she won't go. And I'm afraid to make her more upset than she already is by forcing her."

"Have you called Dr. Nathan?" William Nathan was Esther's internist and she was very fond of him.

"He's on vacation and the referral doctor hasn't called me back."

It was the end of August and many doctors were on vacation.

"I can't watch her all the time," Sam continued, "I just can't. I'm very tired, but I'm afraid to go to sleep. She's not sane anymore and I don't know what she'll do next. I need help. You've got to get back here and help me figure out what to do."

Even though it had appeared for the past few months that Esther's imagination had been working overtime, she had been so funny and good-natured about the odd things going on in her mind that we hadn't taken her notions too seriously. Sam and I may have known by heart the five danger signals of cancer, and probably could have been able to recognize cancer if it had occurred, but we did not know the danger signals of mental illness and did not know that what appeared to be harmless eccentricity one day could blossom into full-blown madness on the next.

I did not know then that the past few months had marked the onset of a serious, insidious condition. Nor did I know that what was happening to my mother is not at all uncommon to older men and women.

I did not know that fifteen to twenty-five percent of all older people have significant symptoms of mental illness.

I did not know that thirty percent of the beds in public mental institutions are occupied by older people.

I did not know that twenty-four percent of all reported suicides are committed by people over the age of sixty.

I did not know that three million older citizens suffer from senility and that one million of them have been confined permanently to mental hospitals and nursing homes.

All I knew then was that something terrible was going on, something I did not understand, something that confused and frightened me. I knew I had to get back to New York City immediately. "I'll be there as soon as I can," I told my father.

2. Esther was sixty-two when she took ill. Her face was unlined and her brown eyes still sparkled. Though her hair had turned gray, she vividly offset the gray with coral lipstick and bright red rouge. She was a high-spirited woman with looks to match.

Esther had always been able to find joy in almost everything. She loved antiques, clothes, window-shopping, new recipes, the movies, the theater. She had the rare quality of being able to both give and receive affection.

News that she was getting new neighbors always delighted her. As soon as they moved in, she rang their bell and introduced herself. She offered them coffee and cake, the use of her telephone, and advice about the best shops in the neighborhood. She liked to meet new people; she liked to make them happy.

The most recent newcomers, however, had turned out to be awful. They left their garbage on the incinerator floor where it would attract bugs; they scattered their newspapers in front of their apartment instead of leaving them stacked neatly in the incinerator closet; they stayed up late, blasting their television set and their stereo system after midnight.

A few months after they moved in, they rang Esther's doorbell with a complaint: *they* accused *her* of being noisy. The accusation offended her; she felt she had been betrayed by people she had befriended, and she could not shake off the bad feeling. She and the new neighbors stopped speaking, except for snappish remarks they made to her in the elevator.

Esther began to brood about what happened; no matter how often we tried to change the subject she would return to it. Then one day while she was alone, she heard voices emanating from the neighbors' apartment. The voices were hostile; Esther was sure they were out to get her.

Soon she began to hear something else: she reported that whenever Sam left the apartment, a sound-effects machine would be turned on, flooding her apartment with a dull but persistent sound.

The neighbors were terrible enough to make us think that there might be some truth to what Esther said;

the alternative—that she was making it up, and therefore was not rational—was too shocking for us even to consider. I realize now that it was too hard for us to acknowledge that someone we loved was losing her hold on reality, so we did not see it, instead entering into Esther's games by humoring her.

She complained to the building superintendent, and then to the landlord. They looked at her quizzically. They could not help laughing and she laughed too. The story sounded ridiculous even to her.

Still Esther insisted that there was a noise. When guests came, she would regale them with stories about the "killer sound-effects machine." People shook their heads in disbelief; then they would all be laughing. And for the moment the problem would vanish in the uproar.

Sam had been retired for two years. During those years Esther and he had considered moving a number of times. Now Sam decided to renew his efforts to move. They would leave the "sound-effects machine" behind them.

After a while they found a lovely apartment on the south shore of Long Island, that pleased them very much. It was within walking distance of Esther's favorite shopping center, a short drive from Sam's golf course and tennis courts, and it bordered a beach where they could while away their summers.

But the prospect of the new apartment did not help Esther shake off her bad feelings.

Sam had once told me that whenever Esther was unhappy, he felt guilty. He loved her desperately and lived to please her; it was his mission to keep her comfortable and happy.

Generally Sam is a very gentle man. When things upset him, he says nothing. However, occasionally the pressure that he imposes upon himself by his silence becomes too much for him, and he erupts in a massive temper tantrum. He was good for one or two of these a year.

Sam had thought that moving would put an end to the problem of the "sound effects." But now the move was less than a week away and Esther was not only continuing to hear the noises but also insisting that a sound truck was behind her. Sam was upset and angry; most of all he was frightened. They were about to move to a bright new apartment to launch a new life. Now he had second thoughts that the move might not make a difference to Esther. That day as they were walking to the grocery store, Esther's irrational movements in the street in order to escape from the "sound truck," her unceasing complaints about the neighbors, and his fear that she might take the "sound effects" with her, finally shattered Sam's control and he began to shout.

I listened carefully as Sam described his outburst over the phone. *"'There aren't any noises! There isn't any sound truck! It's all in your mind! We don't need to move! We don't have to do anything! It's all in your mind!'*

"Through it all, Esther just stared at me," he continued. "She's never looked at me like that before. Now she's convinced that I'm one of them. She told me she doesn't love me anymore. She says I've taken you away and locked you up someplace. You're dead. She has been going on like this for two full days now. I don't know how to stop it. I don't know what to do."

I reassured Sam I would get back to New York as quickly as I could.

As soon as I got off the phone I located Robert. I told him the story and announced that I had to leave immediately. "I'll charter you a plane," he responded, and ordered Joy to phone Bermuda Airport.

We learned that all flights had been canceled for the remainder of the night because of a tropical storm. I was booked onto the first flight the following morning.

Robert and I sat on the porch looking up at the rain clouds forming in the sky. "I know a brilliant psychiatrist, Arthur Barrett," he said. "Perhaps he can be of help."

Barrett was one of the most distinguished psychiatrists in New York City. Joy got him on the phone, Robert chatted with him for a minute or two, then handed the phone to me.

I introduced myself and related Esther's story. The psychiatrist said nothing. "What's wrong with her?" I asked.

"Without seeing her, I really can't make a diagnosis," Dr. Barrett replied. "If you want to make an appointment, I'll be glad to see her. And please feel free to call me if you need me and I'll be glad to give you whatever help I can."

"Thank you. I'm very grateful."

"Don't mention it."

I was about to hang up, but I couldn't resist pressing the doctor once more for some information. "What does it *sound* like to you?"

"How old is your mother?"

"Sixty-two."

"Most of the mental illness in people of that age is caused by neurological disease—brain damage caused by aging."

"*Brain damage?* How can she have brain damage? She just became paranoid about the neighbors, that's all."

"In her case, the paranoia may have been caused by brain damage. When some people get old they develop arthritis or hardening of the arteries. In others the aging process expresses itself as brain damage."

"How is brain damage treated?"

"For the most part it's untreatable."

"Then what do you do?"

"Unfortunately, you have to understand that when some people get old, their sanity slips away because they are suffering from an organic, progressive disease of the brain. There's nothing you can do for these people. There are some nursing homes that specialize in patients like this."

I shook my head in disbelief.

"These can be very difficult moments," Barrett said before hanging up. "Please call me if you need me."

After I got off the phone I repeated the conversation to Robert. He poured me a drink and together we watched the storm envelop the island.

3. Sam had been a physical education teacher before his retirement. Still a fine athlete, whose pleasures revolved around being active and outdoors, at sixty-eight he remained trim and youthful. He was an expert tennis, golf, and handball player.

When I arrived at the apartment Sunday evening, however, I was startled by how old he looked. There were dark circles under his eyes from lack of sleep; his whole face was tensed with anxiety. Most of all, he seemed to have literally shrunk; at that moment, looking down at him, I realized for the first time that I was at least a head taller.

Happy to see me, Sam put his arm around my waist

and pulled me to him. We walked through the small foyer into the living room.

Esther was an inveterate collector. She collected Toby mugs, Victorian greeting cards, miniature antique shoes. There wasn't an inch of available space in the room, but what would be clutter in other people's hands was transformed by her into artfully arranged, colorful displays.

Esther had always loved the theater and she had turned her own home into a glamorous environment that was a witty and fantastical storybook—a never-never land of days gone by.

Esther's friends marveled not only at her ability to collect and decorate with such skill but at her meticulous housekeeping. Each piece in her collection was always sparkling and dustless. Antique dealers marveled at her anticipation of trends: she had collected Tiffany lamps and art deco pieces before they were fashionable. Often she would be offered large sums of money for her collections. Sometimes she had accepted such offers, using the money to finance a new collecting endeavor.

This evening, I saw stacks of cartons everywhere; not one of them was filled.

"We were going to spend the weekend packing for the move to the new apartment next week," Sam explained, "but that was before this happened."

We sat side by side on the couch. "Where's mother?" I asked.

"Asleep." Sam looked away and reached for his pipe. He was reluctant to discuss Esther's condition, and whenever I brought it up he changed the subject. Esther's illness was the reason I had returned to New York, but Sam wanted to avoid the inevitable for the moment, as if not coming to terms with it would make it go away.

He suddenly popped up. "Can I get you anything?"

"I'm fine."

"I'll get you some coffee soda." Never at ease unless he was getting somebody something, he headed into the kitchen anyway.

As I watched him go, I noticed a sudden movement in the corner of the dining room. Esther was hiding in the shadows. I jumped up, went over to her, and gave her a big hug.

She gritted her teeth and clenched her fists. Her body was tense and there was a fierce look in her eyes that I had never seen before.

I led her into the living room, sat her down on the love seat, and held her hand.

"What I've been through!" she whispered, shaking her head in disbelief. Tears rolled down her cheeks.

Suddenly she sat up. "Is he in the kitchen? I've got to get away from him!" She began to tiptoe toward the front door. Then she made a run for it. Sam headed out of the kitchen and I followed after him. Esther turned, sank to her knees, and grabbed my legs. "Please let me out of here," she sobbed. She took my hands and kissed them. I could feel her tears on my fingers. "I've always loved you. I've always done my best for you. I've never asked you for anything. Now I need help! Please, please help me."

I led her back to the couch.

"You don't love me. Get away!" she said as I sat her down.

She was shivering and I put my arm around her shoulders, but she pushed me away with unexpected strength.

I set about trying to distract her until she was tired enough to go to sleep. I told her about my weekend in Bermuda; I told her the plot of *Sgt. Pepper*. We dug out the family scrapbook and slowly surveyed the pictures. Esther proved extremely lucid, almost defiant in her precision as she remembered the details of our family history. She looked at my baby pictures and told me warm, loving stories about my infancy; she then looked at a family picture taken when I was eight and in the third grade. She remembered that the picture was taken the day I had come home from school crying because the kids had made fun of my last name, Katz. Esther had jokingly said, "You obviously need two names; one just won't do. Your middle name is Edward. You can be Henry Edwards and Henry Katz." I had liked the idea, much to her amusement. From that moment on I had made Henry Edwards my pen name and had used it to sign first the compositions and then the short stories I began to write.

She spotted a shot of me, aged thirteen, in a summer camp production of *Damn Yankees,* and recalled her pleasure at my performance. She looked at a photograph of my high school graduation class and remembered not only the names of many of my friends but also funny stories about them.

I knew she was humoring me, hoping to wear me down until I fell asleep, so that she could make her escape.

The ritual went on until almost midnight. There were moments when she would be overcome by a musical urge, and in a loud, lilting voice, she'd sing: "Daisy, Daisy, give me your answer true. I'm half crazy over my love for you . . ."

Sam, yawning and bleary-eyed, sang along with her, hoping that his participation would keep her happy and away from the front door. Finally, he was too exhausted to go on and brought her two tranquilizers.

Esther reluctantly swallowed them. Then Sam, coaxingly, took her by the arm and led her to the bedroom. I followed after them. In the bedroom I kissed her good night. As Esther undressed, she once again began to sing.

Sam poured himself a gin and tonic. He lit up his pipe and sat down next to me. We looked at each other.

"You know, I never thought she was anything like this," Sam said between puffs on his pipe. "I believed what she told me about the noises and didn't question a thing. I was such a fool. I feel I'm to blame. I screamed at her. That's when her mind broke. . . ."

"I should have known better myself. I should have realized how serious this really was. I should have made you get help when she first began to hear the noises."

"You couldn't have known what to do then."

"I should have known. Neither of us is stupid," I said.

We both felt guilty about what we should have known and should have done and we just sat there, too upset to speak, for what seemed like hours.

"Now what are we going to do?" he asked.

"We've got to take her to a hospital tomorrow."

"How long will she be hospitalized?"

"I don't know."

Again we fell silent.

"These have been the three most terrifying days of my life." Sam shook his head in disbelief. "I'm going to try to get some sleep," he said weakly. He stood up and so did I. I put my arm around his waist and walked him to the bedroom. Then I returned to the living room and threw myself down on the sofa, hoping somehow to be able to fall asleep.

I felt Esther's breath against my ear. "I'm going now," she said.

"Go back to bed," I called out in the dark. "In the morning you can go out."

Esther headed for the door, just as Sam came out of the bedroom.

Esther took one look at Sam and once again she burst into tears. She sank to the floor and rocked back and forth.

"Why won't you let me out?" she sobbed.

"I'll call the doctor." Last night Esther had also tried to get out and Sam had called a local medical emergency service. Within a half hour a doctor had arrived and given her an injection of chlorpromazine, a powerful tranquilizer used to restore calm and relieve psychotic behavior.

"No more injections," moaned Esther.

"Why don't we call the police, get an ambulance, and take her to a hospital now." I took the phone from Sam and dialed the police emergency number.

Fifteen minutes later, two policemen rang the doorbell. I informed them that my mother was ill and had to be taken immediately to a hospital. The policemen explained that the law allowed them to take mental patients to only one place—Bellevue, a municipal mental hospital.

One of the cops pulled me aside. "She's a sweet lady," he said. "So what if she's nuts? If it was my mother, I'd never send her to Bellevue. It's filled with junkies and prostitutes. They can get away with anything with a crowd like that. She could be chained up or beaten. Her head could be opened by the time the night is over."

He sounded as if he knew what he was talking about. I thanked him for his advice and told Sam that we would have to wait until morning before making our move.

"Then I'd better call the doctor," he said as he watched the policemen go.

"Why?" asked Esther. "I've done my best."

"Yes, I know you know me," Sam said into the phone. "My wife is ill again. . . . She's trying to go outside. . . . She needs an injection. . . ." Sam hung up the phone and we sat down to wait.

A half hour later, at five-forty that morning, the doctor, an intense young Pakistani, arrived. He looked at Esther, asked only a question or two, then filled a hypodermic needle and rolled up Esther's sleeve. Passively, she allowed the injection to be administered.

"That will be thirty-five dollars," the doctor stated. Sam wrote out a check.

Esther tried to stand up but she could hardly walk. Sam and I propped her between us. The medication was so strong she was almost unconscious when we placed her on the bed. In seconds she was asleep.

Once again, Sam and I sat next to each other on the love seat. I placed my hand in his and squeezed down hard. Once again we sat next to each other in silence. In a few hours we would have to take Esther away. We sat there, waiting, dreading what we would have to do when morning finally arrived.

4. At seven-thirty in the morning, Esther was still in a drugged sleep, but Sam and I were both charged with a kind of desperate manic energy. Sam speedily quartered an orange, poured out a bowl of Cheerios, then put some milk on the table; it was the same breakfast I'd had as a child. He took a kettle from the stove and made me a cup of instant coffee.

"What hospital are we going to?" he asked as he handed me a piece of toast.

I only knew that we had to find Esther the best mental hospital in New York City. I decided to call Dr. Barrett. I dialed his number and explained my problem to his answering service. The operator asked for my number and I was told he would call back immediately.

He did.

When I described Esther's condition to him, he agreed with me that she could not be treated as an outpatient and needed to be hospitalized.

"I'd like to take her to the best mental hospital in New York," I said. "Which would you recommend?"

"Chelsea," he replied. "It has one of the best mental wards of any hospital in the country."

I found the number of the hospital in the phone book and dialed it. Mrs. Griffith, an admitting officer, took my call. For the second time that morning I described Esther's condition. Mrs. Griffith asked to speak to Sam and I handed him the phone.

Sam listened for a moment, then bolted into the bedroom.

"What's the matter?" I called.

"They charge two hundred and ninety dollars a day. They want to know if I can pay for it." He rifled through his bureau, searching for his medical insurance policies. Eventually he emerged from the bedroom, carrying a sheaf of papers.

Sam fumbled with his glasses, then picked up the phone and rattled off his Medicare numbers. He hung up.

"They'll call me back. They want to make sure that

I really have this coverage. They can't admit a patient who does not have medical insurance."

I was astonished; were there people who went around using other people's names and Medicare numbers in order to get themselves admitted to mental hospitals?

We paced back and forth in front of the phone until it finally rang. Mrs. Griffith reported that she had confirmed that Samuel Katz was Samuel Katz, that Samuel Katz's Medicare number belonged to Samuel Katz, and that the Samuel Katz they had on the phone was the Samuel Katz insured by Medicare. Most important, Medicare had guaranteed that it would pay the hospital its full amount directly.

Sam handed the phone back to me.

The admitting officer detailed instructions. Chelsea would take no responsibility for getting Esther to the hospital. It was suggested that I rent a private ambulance. In addition, when we got there, Esther would have to sign herself in voluntarily.

I turned to Sam and repeated Mrs. Griffith's instructions.

"What happens if she doesn't want to get into the ambulance?" Sam asked. "And what happens if she doesn't want to commit herself once she gets there?"

"I don't know," I replied. "I just don't know."

We walked into the bedroom. Esther lay collapsed on the bed. Sam reached down and touched her gently on the shoulder. Tremblingly, she sat up. We sat down beside her. I stroked her face and held her hands as I quietly told her we were going to take her to the hospital. Esther smiled happily. Finally she was going to be let out of her prison. She burst into song.

I then called an ambulance company. Should the driver bring a wheelchair, I was asked, and should he bring his gun? I assured the company that neither was needed. Esther was still singing as I hung up the phone.

Precisely at ten, the ambulance arrived. Esther had on her best coat and her best hat. She wore her favorite jewelry and carried her favorite purse. Dressed for the world's most exciting outing, she eagerly followed us out of the apartment.

Radiant, she climbed into the cab. The ambulance sped off, with Esther singing all the way.

5. A guard at the entrance of Chelsea Hospital directed us to Emily Griffith's office. We walked through the lobby of the dignified, stately building and down a first-floor corridor. Along the way we passed a number of doctors, nurses and technicians, all dressed in long white laboratory coats. Esther smiled and nodded to them and some paused to return the greeting. "What friendly people," she said approvingly.

Mrs. Griffith was waiting for us. First she asked Sam why he had brought Esther to the psychiatric unit of the hospital. Sam recounted it all. "She tries to run out every night. I've found her running in the streets," he said. "No matter what I do, I can't restrain her. She wants to go out and she does."

Then Mrs. Griffith turned to Esther and began to speak to her in a firm, controlled voice. Esther was to tell her why she was going to enter the hospital. She was to write the reason on a form Mrs. Griffith placed before her and she was to sign the form.

Sam stared at Esther, I stared at Esther. We wondered what she would say. Esther said absolutely nothing. Panic-stricken, Sam and I exchanged glances. What were we going to do if she didn't want to sign herself in?

Mrs. Griffith came to the rescue. "*I* think you need to go into the hospital. Now, why do *you* think you do?"

Esther screwed up her face and concentrated on finding the answer.

"I think you need a rest," said Mrs. Griffith.

Esther smiled sweetly. She nodded her head in agreement.

"Now you tell me: why do you think you should go into the hospital?"

Esther thought for a while. And then she had it. "I'm a bastard," she said softly. "I'm going into the hospital to get a birth certificate." Esther's birth had never been registered and a birth certificate had not been issued until she began to attend school. Often she had been teased about it. "I've never been a good wife and mother," she continued, "because I was illegitimate."

"Write your reason on this form right here." Mrs. Griffith pointed to the appropriate space.

Slowly, Esther printed: "I'm . . . a . . . bastard." She looked at Sam and began to weep. "You should never have married a bastard. I told you it would only bring you trouble."

Sam wanted to comfort her; he also knew that nothing he said could help. His eyes filled with tears.

"Now," said Mrs. Griffith, "sign your name."

Esther slowly wrote her maiden name: "Esther Roberta Korman." She looked up at Mrs. Griffith. "I didn't write my married name," she explained, "because I haven't been a good wife."

With that the formalities were over. Esther Roberta Korman Katz had committed herself to Chelsea Hospital's psychiatric ward.

Mrs. Griffith picked up her phone, buzzed for an orderly, then turned to Esther. "Now we're going to take you upstairs so you can have your rest."

Esther got up. She smiled at Mrs. Griffith. "I'm only happy in hospitals," she said. "This is the seventh time I've gone to the hospital, and I've had a good time every single time."

The orderly appeared, picked up Esther's bags, and we all turned and filed out to the elevator.

When we got off the elevator, we found ourselves facing a large steel door. The orderly rang the doorbell. A guard stared out the peephole at him and then the door was opened. It had not dawned on me until then that Esther would be kept under lock and key.

The orderly introduced us to Rose, a bright-eyed teenager who was a trainee. We walked behind Rose past the patients' lounge as she escorted Esther to her room.

I noticed that all the furnishings were as shabby and faded as the lobby had been ornate. We passed a few patients marching mechanically up and down the corridors. Their eyes were vacant; they stared straight ahead; some muttered to themselves. They looked as if they were heavily sedated.

Rose began to help Esther unpack and undress. Sam stood there wanting to make contact with his wife, but she had shut him out. She wanted to be rid of us, and all we could do was oblige. Rose suggested that we go to the nurses' station in the center of the floor to meet Esther's doctor.

We followed her instructions. At the nurses' station we met the nurse in charge, Mrs. Stanton, who in turn introduced us to Esther's doctor, a man named Jonathan Conrad.

Dr. Conrad was surrounded by a group of patients. Some called his name; others reached out to touch him.

Everywhere he turned, someone wanted his attention, and he could hardly keep up.

"We'll have a meeting," he told us, and he started to walk away.

"When?" I called after him.

"I don't know yet. I have to study the case."

"Should I call you in the morning?"

"Fine. I'll talk to you tomorrow." He gave us a quick nod and then he hurried down the hall.

Before leaving, Sam wanted to look in on Esther one more time.

"Daisy, Daisy, give me your answer true," she sang as she sat up in her new bed.

We said goodbye, but she ignored us. Finally we left. At the steel door we identified ourselves to the guard. He studied us for a moment, assuring himself that we were not patients trying to make a getaway, and then he opened it. Suddenly, we were on the outside, and Esther had been locked inside.

Stunned, we said nothing in the elevator. Nor did we say anything as we left the hospital and walked down the street. Sam's eyes were filled with tears. So were mine. We were both wrecks, but I was determined to stay in control. I didn't want to burden him with my despair; he had enough of his own. Silently, as we walked, Sam kept chastising himself for yelling at Esther. I silently kept blaming myself for not intervening earlier. And both of us wondered if we had waited too long.

Finally, breaking the silence, I said, "Chelsea has the best mental facilities in the city. The doctors have to know what they're doing. I think they are going to do a fine job of helping her." The words sounded hollow, but Sam smiled appreciatively.

I announced that I was hungry and we headed for a coffee shop to get some lunch.

"I'm never going to give up hope, no matter what happens," he said quietly as we settled into a booth. Then he drifted off again. "I can't believe this is happening to us," he said suddenly.

Neither could I.

That night I called Dr. Barrett. "Esther's doctor is a resident," I told him.

"Chelsea is a teaching hospital," said Barrett. "That's one reason why it's so special. New doctors train there because it's such a good hospital."

"Isn't he too young to have the experience to deal with my mother?"

"Every move he makes is watched, evaluated and supervised by a highly experienced team. You'll see. At Chelsea, you don't get one doctor—you get a doctor who represents an entire team. You'll be amazed and delighted by what her psychiatrists do," said Barrett. "If they can't help, no one can."

6. Esther Roberta Korman was born on May 23, 1914, in the back room of her parents' theatrical costume workshop in the Borough Hall section of Brooklyn. She was delivered by the neighborhood doctor, an elderly, cantankerous man who liked to take a drink or two named Benjamin Evans. Because Evans did not register Esther's birth, no birth certificate was issued. However, when Esther began to go to school, the oversight was discovered and the necessary documentation was requested and issued. Despite this prosaic reality, Esther's lack of a birth certificate became permanently enshrined in family lore.

She was the daughter of Beckie Einhorn and Max Korman. Beckie and Max had met on Manhattan's Lower East Side, where they lived in adjoining tenements. Max was a young actor in a Jewish theatrical company; Beckie was a seamstress.

Beckie was hard-working, serious and ambitious. Max was hardly ever serious about anything. They were the proverbial case of opposites irresistibly attracted to each other.

The Kormans had three children. The oldest, Ceil, was a musical prodigy, who, by the time she was five, could play a complete selection of Italian folk songs on the mandolin. Ceil became a professional when she won the first Metropolitan Opera audition of the air and was given a weekly job playing the violin on the radio. The middle child, Frank, was headstrong and argumentative. A practicing socialist, he was determined to become a lawyer and then use the law to eliminate the inequities in the society into which he had been born.

Working day and night, Beckie sewed nurses' uniforms, stage costumes, and athletic uniforms, while Max pressed pants, bottled bootleg liquor, played practical jokes, sang his songs, and gambled. Together the Kormans made enough money to send Frank to law school and Ceil abroad to study with a distinguished violin teacher.

Beckie's only problem was her "baby," Esther, who was twelve years younger than Frank and fifteen years younger than Ceil. Esther was a beautiful girl with sparkling brown eyes and shiny black curls. Her skin was so fine and smooth it seemed translucent. Beckie doted on her, dominating and overprotecting her, not only because she was so lovely but also because she displayed no particular aptitude for anything except having fun.

The best of friends, Max and his daughter Esther were inseparable. They went everywhere together—to the circus and to the movies, to vaudeville houses, auctions, the opera. Max would rent a horse-drawn carriage and together they would spend the afternoon touring the farmlands of Brooklyn.

One day Max was summoned to school because Esther had misbehaved. He was not angry at his daughter, however; the school was undoubtedly the culprit.

"Your job is not to break my daughter's spirit," he announced angrily to the principal. "Your job is to encourage it."

I always believed that nothing would break Esther's spirit. Nothing did until she became mentally ill.

Sam had also come from an extremely hard-working family. His parents—Rose, a seamstress, and Aaron, a clothing machine operator—had migrated from Russia in 1914. Aaron had had a feeling that war was imminent; he also refused to live in a country that would allow only ten percent of its Jewish population to go to college.

Because their funds were meager, the Katzes could afford to obtain the necessary documents and pay for the passage of only two of their four children. They desperately tried to raise more money but couldn't. Eventually they made the painful decision to take their two youngest, two-year-old Belle and five-year-old Sam, work as hard as they could in their new homeland, and then send for seven-year-old Lillian and nine-year-old Max, whom they left in the care of relatives.

Rose, Aaron, Sam and Belle set off by train to Hamburg. In Hamburg, they boarded the boat for America. For twenty-six difficult days they were packed into steerage with a horde of other Russian emigrants. The food was so terrible that Aaron tipped the cook to get better scraps of dried herring and salted bread for his wife and children. Finally, the boat docked in Galveston, Texas, where Aaron had been told he had the best chance of finding a job. But the Russian-speaking Jewish quartet found it rough going in the southern port city, so they moved on to Kansas City, where they also had no luck. Next they headed to New York City, eventually settling in Brooklyn.

Because their parents worked a long, hard week, the children were put in charge of the house. At an early age, the immigrant ethic of long hours and hard work was ingrained in each of them.

The minute his chores were over, Sam ran to the schoolyard. He was a natural athlete, who loved to play stickball, punchball, and cat-of-nine-tails. Semiprofessional baseball teams competed at St. Agatha's Field, just a few short blocks from his home; on the weekends, kids would perch behind the St. Agatha's fence, waiting for a foul ball to come sailing into their gloves. Any kid who caught a foul ball was allowed in to see the game for nothing. Every Saturday and Sunday morning, Sam would take his place behind the fence, hoping to catch the ball, and many times he did. He loved baseball more than anything.

At the end of the year, enough money had been saved to bring Lillian and Max to the United States. Now the three older children went to school together and then each worked at a number of part-time jobs to help maintain the family. Sam became an all-star athlete, and at his high school graduation was awarded a letter for every sport offered by the school.

He decided to attend New York University to become a teacher of physical education. To pay for his tuition, he spent his summers working as a waiter and tennis instructor in children's summer camps, his evenings sorting letters in the post office, and his weekends taking on a number of odd jobs—including stock boy in a bathrobe house and runner for a brokerage.

Upon graduation he became a substitute teacher and began preparing for the regular licensing examination. If he passed it, he would get a permanent job in one of the city's public high schools. Once he had that job, he planned to marry and start a family.

Every Sunday morning, Sam played handball at the nearby Jewish Community House. His doubles partner was Esther's brother, Frank. Frank liked Sam, he liked his seriousness, his dedication to hard work, his desire to have a stable, successful life. He thought Sam just might be the steadying influence his younger sister needed.

Frank invited Sam to dinner. The attraction between the fun-loving young woman and the serious young man was immediate. Even though he didn't have much cash to spare, Sam invited Esther on a posh Saturday night date: they traveled to Broadway to see Loretta Young in *The Unguarded Hour* at the Capitol Theatre. Afterward they went to the chic Central Park Theatre Hotel and had dinner while they were serenaded by strolling musicians. By the end of the evening they were holding hands.

Sam decided not to propose marriage until he passed the regular licensing examination and had a secure job. These were the Depression years and he believed that without security he would have no future. Because so many people wanted teaching jobs and none was available, the licensing examination was postponed indefinitely. Sam had been a substitute teacher for three years and waited almost two years more before the test for permanent teachers was announced. Sam took it, then waited months for the results. One morning when he went to the mailbox, he found the letter he was waiting for—the letter informing him that he had passed.

That afternoon he proposed to Esther and she accepted.

They were married on April 5, 1938, and in September Sam began his permanent teaching career at East New York Vocational High School in Brooklyn. I was born five years later.

7. The marriage was a happy one and Frank's prediction that marriage would steady Esther appeared to have come true.

I was an only child, my birth preceded by one miscarriage and followed by two more. Immediately after my birth, Esther had an attack of appendicitis. Her appendix burst, and she developed severe peritonitis. She was hospitalized for months and almost died.

In the course of years, she also underwent the removal of a spinal cyst, a complete hysterectomy, and the removal of her gall bladder. Through it all she maintained her ebullience and her sense of humor. And Sam continued to be the perfect gentleman: quiet, soft-spoken, polite, decent, loyal, self-sacrificing. Together they built a network of devoted friends, who were delighted by Esther's love of life and her colorful ways and made secure by Sam's gentleness and charm. Like Beckie and Max, my parents were opposites who were suited to each other.

Sam taught school every day, he coached the high school baseball team in the afternoons, he ran a community center in the evenings, he worked in children's camps every summer. For his entire working life he managed four jobs in order to make Esther and me as comfortable as he could.

My childhood was a relatively happy one; I always received plenty of affection and attention. Sam could not afford to send me to an out-of-town college and after high school I continued to live at home while I attended Brooklyn College. My father had encouraged me to become a teacher and after graduation I joined the school system as a teacher of English. Eight years later, however, I made the decision to become a full-time writer.

Esther and Sam were uneasy. Their Depression mentality demanded that I have a job. Yet they also maintained a policy of noninterference where I was concerned. They became philosophical, and decided that what made me happy made them happy too. I wrote and published a novel; then I wrote a television special. Finally, I began to write popular-music criticism, eventually becoming a weekly contributor to the Arts and Leisure section of *The New York Times.* Then I landed the opportunity to write *Sgt. Pepper.*

Esther and Sam were delighted. We had always been relatively close, speaking on the phone once or twice a week, seeing each other once or twice a month. We had faced no real crises, and had few unpleasant moments. Even Esther's seven hospitalizations had been handled with a sense of humor. The three of us prided ourselves individually on being able to take care of ourselves without inconveniencing one another—though each of us knew the others would be there if and when we needed them.

After thirty-eight years in the New York City school system, Sam decided to file for retirement at the age of sixty-seven.

When the retirement was granted, a small group of close friends gathered for a celebratory dinner. At the height of it, Esther climbed on a chair to propose a toast.

"Sam has worked long and hard," she said, "and finally we've got the time and money to have some fun."

Everybody applauded and assumed that fun was what they would have.

For almost their entire married life, Sam's work schedule had kept Sam and Esther apart all day every day, as well as almost every evening. Now they were never apart. Married thirty-eight years, they now had to learn to live with each other on a full-time basis.

Sam, always full of boundless energy, was trained to do a job, but suddenly he was a man with no job to do. He would pop up at dawn, wash, eat breakfast, do the dishes, tidy the apartment, and be ready to begin his day. He would play tennis or golf and come home with energy to spare. After lunch he and Esther would go out together. They would shop, go to the library, attend antique fairs and auctions.

Esther, equally energetic, utilized her energies to window-shop, visit her favorite storekeepers and antique dealers, gossip, keep up with her friends, search out things that would be amusing to do.

They would set out each afternoon, Sam marching straight ahead. Soon Esther was blocks behind. Sam would turn around, see Esther entranced by a window display, and have to backtrack. It would happen time and time again, and Sam, becoming impatient, would continually urge Esther to hurry up. They were people with different rhythms and their rhythms were not in synch.

"He's always underfoot," Esther would moan. "Suddenly I can't do a thing."

Together twenty-four hours a day, seven days a week, they began to complain that they had run out of things to do and places to go. Their friends were all retiring to Florida or California, leaving them alone. Esther's brother and sister were dead. And Sam's only surviving sister had also gone to Florida. They had no grandchildren and could not play the role of loving grandparents. They had assumed that with retirement would come relaxation and fun; instead, they were trapped in the most stress-filled transition of their lives.

Then Sam decided to move to Florida. As they toured the state, Esther's objections grew. The condominiums they could afford were little cramped spaces in which Esther did not feel comfortable. She also dreaded spending the hot summers in even hotter Florida. But as a retired couple on a fixed income, they felt they could not afford to travel north during the summer as many others could, and would have no alternative but to stay and face the heat.

Esther was also dismayed as she toured the retirement villages. Neither Sam nor she felt like "senior citizens" and she was accustomed to living in buildings where there was a normal range of ages.

"I can't do it," she told Sam as she looked around. "I guess I'm just not ready to accept what Florida means."

Sam did not argue. It was not his job to argue. Sitting side by side on the plane going home, they had nothing to say to each other. They had no idea of what they would do now. But they knew they would have to do something. After all, they had always believed that retirement would be their reward for thirty-eight years of hard work. Now they were retired and the reward had still not come.

Esther confessed her dream to me: Sam and she would move to Manhattan.

"We can't afford Manhattan," Sam said emphatically. "But," he added, "we should move. We'll find someplace pretty to move to, with lots of things to do."

Each morning after breakfast, they set out to find that new place to live. They scoured New Jersey, Connecticut, Westchester, and were amazed by the prices of the homes they liked.

Finally, to pacify Esther, Sam agreed to try Manhattan.

I accompanied them as they inspected studio apartments—tiny one-room spaces in luxury apartment houses—as well as larger apartments on blocks that were unsafe to walk along. Everywhere the rents were exorbitant.

The Manhattan experience proved the final discouragement, and Sam announced that the search was over. Sadly, they returned home, realizing that they just had no other options.

They did not look again until Esther had her problems with the neighbors. This time their luck changed. They found a lovely, reasonable apartment in a neighborhood they liked. At the time they found it, Sam could never have guessed that he would be moving alone.

8.

At eleven the morning after Esther committed herself, Dr. Conrad called me, "I have some bad news for you," he said. "Last night, your mother took a bad fall. Her ankle is shattered in three places."

It seemed absurd to me. No one breaks her ankle on the day she checks into a mental hospital. This was the sort of thing that happened on television, not in real life. "Why wasn't she watched?" I asked angrily. "You knew we put her in the hospital because she wandered at night."

"We do the best we can. But you can never predict what will happen with mental patients. Unfortunately, there can be unpleasant surprises."

"Is she all right? Is she in pain?"

"She's under sedation," Conrad replied. "Do you want to call your father or shall I?"

"I will," I said, and hung up.

I sat for a while trying to get control of myself and figure out how to tell Sam. At last I felt calm enough to call and give him the news. He was frantic. We both set out for the hospital immediately.

An hour later we met at the front entrance. We got our visitors' passes and headed for Esther's room.

A restraining jacket held Esther firmly in bed. Her leg was in a cast up to her knee. We called her name but she did not respond. She said nothing and stared into space. She was under heavy sedation. I don't know what disturbed me more—the sight of the cast or the unnatural stillness of her face and eyes.

Sam reached down and touched Esther's arm. There was no response. He kissed her forehead. She stared up, comprehending nothing, not even blinking.

Sam couldn't bear it. He turned and stepped out of the room.

"Let's talk to Dr. Conrad," I suggested. Sam followed me as we walked to the nurses' station in the center of the corridor.

"I'm Mr. Katz," Sam gently reminded Mrs. Stanton. "My wife is Mrs. Katz. . . ."

"I know. The one with the leg. We're looking after her."

"What happened?" I asked.

"I'm sorry. I wasn't on duty at that time. You'll have to talk to Dr. Conrad."

"Where is he?"

"He isn't on the floor now. The best way to reach him is to phone him and leave a message. He'll call you back when he has time." Mrs. Stanton turned away.

Sam looked bewildered. We both stood there, stunned. I was just beginning to realize that to the hospital, Esther was not Esther, a unique human being, but merely one of many patients, one of many case numbers.

I took Sam by the arm and we walked back to Esther's room. Her eyes were still wide open and blank. As she breathed, she emitted a slight wheeze.

Sam and I stared at her. Finally, we kissed her good-bye and left.

"This is going to be a long one," Sam said wearily as we walked down the street.

At lunch, though he rarely drank, Sam ordered gin and tonics for both of us. He gulped his down, then ordered another.

"What are you going to do about moving?" I asked. "Can you get an extension?"

"I went to the landlord and told him that Esther was in the hospital. It seems crazy to move now, doesn't it? We've been tenants in that building for nineteen years, and do you know what? He said we had to get out. Our apartment had already been rented."

"I don't believe it. How much time do you have?"

"Three days."

We fell silent.

"What's wrong with her?" Sam suddenly asked. "If we knew what was wrong with her, we'd have some idea of what can be done."

"I'm sure we'll find out as soon as they've some information to give us."

"But I want to know now," said Sam. "I have to know *now*."

We finished our meal; Sam paid the check. As we left, I sensed that he did not want to go home.

"We've always been father and son," he said as we began to walk down the street. "Now we're an army, an army of two. The job of this army is to help Esther and protect her, no matter how badly each of us feels."

"You know I'll do everything that has to be done."

"Nothing can ever be predicted," Sam said. "By all rights, Esther and I should be living happily in Florida. Now she's in the hospital, I'm moving to Long Island, and you're a movie writer commuting between New York, Los Angeles and Bermuda." He shook his head. "I never expected all of these surprises."

"Neither did I," I said, feeling equally dislocated.

"You did the right thing," Sam said suddenly.

"What did I do?"

"You refused to continue doing what you didn't want to do when you finally decided what you wanted. You had the guts to leave the school system. That made me happy."

"Weren't you concerned that I wouldn't be able to make a living?"

"You were moving forward. That's all I cared about."

"What about the fact that I got involved with rock music?"

Sam shrugged. "I didn't know anything about it, but the fact that you know something about it is what gave you your chance. It gave you an opportunity to establish yourself. That's how you got to write *Sgt. Pepper.* And that's made me the proudest of all."

Moments like this were rare and touching, for my father was a man who did not find it easy to share his deepest feelings.

That night we began to pack all of Esther's many treasured possessions. Sam wanted none of them broken and he did not trust the moving men to do the job properly. So for hours we wrapped Esther's prizes in pieces of newspaper, then placed them in cartons.

For the next three days we drove back and forth to the new apartment, conveying the cartons. After the last one had been moved, the movers came for the furniture.

In his new apartment, Sam unpacked the cartons. In these unfamiliar surroundings, without his wife, Sam attempted to reassure himself by arranging the furniture and objects as closely as possible to the way they had been arranged before.

When the last picture was finally in place, he sat down to wait and wonder when—or if—his wife would ever be well enough to see their new home.

9. It took me a week to find Dr. Conrad, who had not returned any of my phone calls.

"What exactly is wrong with my mother?" I asked him.

"There are two classifications of mental disorders,"

Conrad told me, "organic mental disorders, which are usually related to aging of the brain, and functional mental disorders, which are usually psychological in origin. Knowing whether your mother is suffering from an organic or a functional mental disorder is crucial. This diagnosis will determine her entire course of treatment."

"When will you know?" I asked.

"More than fifty percent of all geriatric patients—patients over sixty-five—suffer from some form of organic brain syndrome. . . ."

"A doctor suggested that she had brain damage," I said, "but I still find it impossible to believe."

"To support a diagnosis of organic brain syndrome, we have to prove that a specific organic factor is at the root of her disturbance. Does she have a disease like arteriosclerosis, which has caused this condition? Or is there something wrong with the brain itself? Is there a tumor, for example, or a lesion?

"We have to give her a great many tests and they take time. As soon as I get the neurology report, I'll let you know."

Once again he sped off.

I spotted Mrs. Stanton at the nurses' station, but knew she wouldn't tell me a thing. None of the nurses would.

I sat in Esther's room for a while, watching her as she lay staring into space. Then I headed for the patients' lounge.

On the way I saw Rose, the trainee who had helped unpack Esther's things, carrying a tray into a room. I reached into my wallet, took out a ten-dollar bill, and waited for her to come out.

"This is for you," I said, "for being so helpful to my mother."

"Thank you," she said as she took the money. "I'm

sorry about your mother. She's a nice lady."

"How did my mother break her ankle?" I asked.

"She took a bad fall."

"What was she doing?"

"She was very upset about being here. She was walking up and down the halls. Then she was listening to the walls. I asked her what she was doing. She said she was looking for Norma Shearer. Then she just slipped. It was very nasty."

Rose shook her head in disbelief. "The most amazing thing about it was that she didn't hurt at all. She didn't cry or nothing. I couldn't believe it, but she didn't feel any pain. There was even a smile on her face. She even tried to get up and walk on her broken foot. I couldn't believe it. Isn't that amazing?"

"Why didn't she feel any pain? Was she on medication?" I asked.

"She had had a big injection of chlorpromazine."

I remembered how the small dosage of chlorpromazine that night at home had instantly knocked her out. Suppose she had been too full of chlorpromazine to feel the pain of her ankle crumbling beneath her? But if that was the case, why had she been allowed to wander around?

This was the best mental ward in any hospital in New York City. At that moment it seemed inconceivable to me that Esther had been either overdosed or left unsupervised. What I wanted to believe, what I *had* to believe, was that Conrad would come up with an expert diagnosis and a precise cure, just as I wanted to believe that Mrs. Stanton and the other nurses were devoted, loving human beings. I wanted to believe that Esther was in safe, expert hands.

I found the ward cold and unfriendly, but it seemed inconceivable to me that the psychiatrists weren't competent.

10. The next day, Sam and I met with Esther's orthopedist, Dr. Richard Fiske. "Mrs. Katz will have to spend four weeks in the knee-length cast," he told us. "At the end of that time, the cast will be shortened to one that rises just a few inches above her ankle. She will have to remain in that cast for another four weeks."

More confused than ever, Esther now had absolutely no idea of where she was or why she was there. Nor could she accept the fact that her ankle was broken. Even though the cast was very heavy, as soon as she was returned to her room she tried to climb out of bed, cast and all. The decision was made to keep her restrained around the clock.

"Untie me. Please, please untie me," was all she would say to Sam and me when we visited her. She looked at us pleadingly, but though she was in great distress, we dared not touch the straps.

Sam paced back and forth. Occasionally he stopped and stared out the window at the streets below. Then he turned and looked at Esther. "Untie me," she repeated. "Please untie me."

I reached over to wipe Esther's sweating brow and I smelled urine.

I headed for the nurses' station to tell Mrs. Stanton that her bedding needed to be changed.

The nurse did not look pleased. "We'll change her," she told me abruptly.

"When?"

"Soon."

I headed back to the room.

"Untie me," Esther begged as soon as she saw me again.

Sam and I sat on a bench in front of Esther's room. "Untie me. Untie me," she called out over and over again. We sat there for an hour. Finally a nurse came down the hall.

Esther's sheets were changed and she was tied back into the bed. Immediately she pulled against the restrainers. When she had no luck, she tried to roll back and forth in an attempt to gather enough momentum to roll over the sides of the bed onto the floor.

The last thing we heard as the guard unlocked the door for us was Esther banging against the sides of her bed, trying to get free.

We visited her every day. We brought her magazines and candy, which she ignored, and toilet articles, which she did not use. Sometimes she just lay there and said nothing; on other occasions, she could make some sense; usually she ordered us out of her room or pretended she was asleep.

We each tried to reach Dr. Conrad. Only he could tell us the results of the tests Esther had been given. But he never called us back. Nobody else on the staff knew when we would get the results and our concern meant absolutely nothing to them. Their attitude seemed to be: *Your mother is a mental patient who is over sixty years of age. Unfortunately, there's not much anybody can do in such a difficult situation. Nonetheless, when the doctor is ready, he will tell you whatever he can.*

So we waited. And we continued to visit Esther, and as we watched her our fears continued to grow. Not only did she refuse to take care of herself, but her personal care did not seem of much concern to the hospital staff. Sometimes her breath seemed sour; often her teeth weren't brushed, and there was also a smell of urine about her.

Occasionally a nurse would take Esther for a wheelchair ride and leave the chair in the hall. "It's good for her to be around other people," I would be told. She would be left to sit for hours in the hall, lost in her own world.

We begged and cajoled the nurses and gave them gifts and money in an attempt to get them to take better care of Esther. They promised they would look after her, but there was not much evidence that they did more than the minimum.

Rose told me that Esther's condition distressed her. "You know why? Because she won't use the bedpan. When a patient doesn't, they don't let her go home. Then she's either got to stay in the hospital or be sent to an institution. That's all you can do with them when they insist on wetting their bed."

"But she insists she calls for a bedpan and no one brings her one."

"Sometimes you have to wait—but bringing a bedpan is the one thing they really try to do as quickly as they can."

During her second week in the hospital Esther was still delusional, but now she did a lot of talking—to anybody. Often she did not know who we were, but that did not stop her from talking to us.

She told us first that she was about to marry a rich man; somehow she had been sent to this strange place to prepare for the wedding. In her mind she had transformed everyone in the hospital into a part of her family.

A patient would walk down the hall and Esther would stare out at him. "Mama, it's Esther," she would call out, but her "mother" didn't respond. Why did her mother ignore her? she asked me. Why did they all ignore her? Why did they keep her tied to her bed?

When we would tell her that her ankle was broken, she'd insist that it wasn't true. We were all liars, she told us, and she hated us. Whenever the nurses touched her, she said, she could feel their contempt.

So day after day, night after night, she twisted and turned, trying to get free.

Then it dawned on her. She had been lied to—lied to for a reason. No one believed she was strong enough to face the truth: she had been hospitalized because she had cancer and now she was undergoing the preparation for surgery.

But that didn't make any sense, either. Nothing anybody did made any sense. Every so often Dr. Conrad asked her a series of questions designed to test whether or not she was rational: "Where are you now?" he would ask her. "What day is this? . . . How old are you? . . . What is your birthday? . . . Who is the President of the United States?"

She hated him and she hated his questions. Why had he asked her such stupid questions? Was that any way for a doctor to behave?

She kept trying to figure out where she was and why she was tied up. She had another idea: this was no hospital; it was hell. Yet it was hard to believe that the devil liked to ask you who the President was. It was hard to believe that his assistants would pretend they were nurses. They were a deceitful lot and Esther hated them all.

Still, she needed them because they controlled the bedpan. All day long she would ring the bell on the night table next to her bed, and if she was lucky one of them would bring her a bedpan. There were times, though, when she would be ignored no matter how hard and long she rang.

One day after her ringing had been ignored for what

seemed to her to be a particularly long time, she could not stand it any longer. In a fit of superhuman strength, she pulled herself free from the restraining jacket. She jumped from her bed, cracking the cast in the process, and hurriedly dressed herself. Limping speedily down the hall, she got as far as the locked door before she was surrounded by nurses.

Once again she was tied up and left to rot in "hell," ringing her bell and begging for a bedpan that might or might not come.

11. Day after day, Sam repeated the same question he had asked the doctor on the second day of Esther's hospitalization: What is really wrong with her?

And for nineteen long days all I could reply was that I was sure Dr. Conrad would tell us as soon as the tests were completed.

"Why is it taking so long to find out what's going on?" Sam kept asking me.

"I don't know," I kept repeating. All I did know was that the ward moved at its own speed, oblivious of the feelings of anyone. A day to them was just another day; to us a day without any information was another day of anguish.

Esther's internist, Dr. Nathan, had returned from his vacation and I called to tell him what had happened to Esther. He was shocked. He, too, believed that he had been guilty of ignoring the distress signals that Esther had been sending during the past year. I told him about her broken ankle.

"You always start older people on extremely small doses of medication and watch their reactions before you dare try them on something stronger," he said firmly. "You don't just give them a big shot of chlorpromazine." He thought for a second, then he suddenly changed his tone. "But neither you nor I knows exactly what did happen. Painful as it is to realize, she may have just had an unavoidable accident." He tried to reassure me by telling me that Chelsea undoubtedly would do a banner job. He also asked me to have Conrad call him.

I told him I would—if Conrad ever called me.

On the nineteenth day of Esther's hospitalization he did, and said that he would like to meet with Sam and me.

When we entered his office, the young psychiatrist was there along with Margaret Carr, a social worker assigned to the case. He sat behind his desk, studying a stack of medical reports.

"What are your reactions to the past three weeks?" he began.

Sam and I spoke at once, a litany of complaints pouring forth from us. There had been no communication, no explanations, no information; the nurses were not looking after Esther; she had been left unsupervised and she had shattered her ankle as a result of their negligence. Most of all, she was getting worse. *How was the hospital going to stop her from getting worse?*

Conrad listened and said nothing. "Your feelings are understandable in a situation like this," he finally replied. He turned toward Sam. "I've told your son that the most common mental illness among older people is organic brain syndrome. It is the disease we have to check for first. We have spent the past three weeks trying to determine whether Mrs. Katz has organic brain syndrome. We've given her a complete physical examination, an electroencephalogram, a series of X rays of the brain."

"What have you discovered?"

"Her results were all in the normal range."

Sam and I looked quizzically at each other. "Then she doesn't have organic brain syndrome," I stated. "What does she have?"

"Every morning the floor chief has a meeting with the staff of the entire floor. All the residents, the nurses and the aides meet together every day to discuss each and every case. We think Mrs. Katz could have a functional disorder. There could also be enough organicity to encourage her condition but not enough to turn up on the tests. To play it safe, we've decided to treat her illness as both a functional and an organic disorder. I'm dealing with the presumed organic aspects of her illness by treating her with a medication named haloperidol."

"What does haloperidol do?" I asked.

"Haloperidol is classified as an antipsychotic. It is an extremely strong tranquilizer that restores emotional calm. It relieves anxiety, agitation and psychotic behavior. It is believed that haloperidol controls the action of dopamine, a compound in the brain that helps regulate nerve impulse transmissions. The haloperidol helps correct any imbalance that might have been the cause of her psychotic behavior."

"If it's helping," said Sam, "why is she lying there like a dead woman?"

"That's because the drug has begun to take effect."

Once again Sam and I looked over at each other. "I don't understand," I exclaimed.

"The drug is helping clear her mind, leaving her with the thoughts and feelings she couldn't deal with in the first place. The thoughts and feelings that originally made her sick have returned. Once again she cannot deal with them, so now she's retreated into depression. What you're looking at is an extremely depressed woman."

"What are you going to do about this depression?"

"Normally I'd prescribe an antidepressant, but anti-depressants can decrease the effectiveness of antihypertensive medication. Mrs. Katz's blood pressure is already high; if she were given antidepressant medication, it could go even higher. I can't risk that, so I'm not going to use any. The haloperidol will relieve the psychotic symptoms; to lift the depression, we've got to find the cause of it without relying on medication. We've got to give Mrs. Katz some insights into what originally upset her and what is depressing her now."

"I want to make sure I've got this straight," I said. "You've given my mother a medication that has relieved her of the psychotic symptoms . . ."

"Relieved her of enough of her psychotic symptoms . . ."

"Relieved her of enough of her psychotic symptoms to allow her to touch base with the problems that originally made her ill. Now she's become depressed but she can't take antidepressant medication because of high blood pressure . . ."

"So we're going to use therapy."

"Therapy?"

"Your father and your mother and I will start a series of 'family meetings.' We'll do the best we can at these meetings to help Mrs. Katz understand her underlying problems—the problems that made her sick in the first place."

Sam looked uncomfortable. It was hard for him to accept the notion that Esther had "underlying problems." They had been married for thirty-eight years and for thirty-eight years he had devotedly loved and cared for her. How could she have "underlying problems"? But he was willing to do anything to help.

"To prepare for these meetings, I've got to get some information." Dr. Conrad looked at Sam. "I'm going to ask you some questions," he said.

"What would you like to know?" asked Sam.

"How do you two get along?"

Sam sketched in a picture of two contented people struck by a series of problems precipitated by Sam's retirement.

"What was your money situation like?"

Sam related that they were capable of living nicely but not extravagantly.

"Were there any drinking problems? . . . Drug problems? . . . Valium abuse?"

"No."

"Was there another woman?"

"No," Sam said with astonishment. "Perhaps in the course of our marriage I've been too overprotective. Perhaps I've been too overbearing; I did lose my temper; but I don't believe that could possibly be the cause of what has happened."

"Of course not. These conditions develop over a long period of time, with one incident precipitating the breakdown. Now, that's enough for today," said Conrad. "Is there anything else either of you wants to discuss?"

"Her care distresses us," I replied. "For example, do you think you could have her teeth brushed?"

"I'll look into that."

"I want to keep in close touch with you," I continued. "After this meeting I'm afraid you'll disappear again and I'll call you and call you and you won't call back."

"Your father will be seeing me at least once a week at our family meetings."

"Once a week? You don't think you are going to cure her by meeting only *once a week?* At that rate these meetings could go on forever."

Conrad sighed. Even though it was still morning, he suddenly looked exhausted. "Your mother is seriously ill in an area about which we know very little. She has an illness that is just as serious and as bewildering as cancer. If she had cancer, would you be angry because the hospital had devoted three weeks to testing her before they came to any conclusions about a diagnosis and course of treatment? If she had cancer and she spent six months or a year in the hospital getting weekly treatments, would you complain about the passage of time in that case?

"Treating your mother's illness is going to take time. And only time is going to tell us if anything works at all. The entire hospital is at her disposal and a large group of professionals deals with her case every single day. But all any of us can really do is the best we can, and watch and wait and hope that something we do turns her condition around."

Conrad stood up. "I'll see you a week from today, next Monday morning at ten. Then we'll have our first session," he said to Sam. The meeting was over. Conrad scooped up his papers and hurried out the door.

12. "Do you really understand what's wrong with Esther?" Sam asked me after the meeting.

I had listened very carefully to what Conrad had to say. He had said that Esther "could have a functional disorder" with "enough organicity to encourage her condition."

"I heard what Conrad had to say," I replied, "but I'm no expert and can't tell whether he's right or wrong. I'm going to do some checking on my own."

That night I called Dr. Barrett, summarized Conrad's diagnosis, and asked Barrett his opinion of it.

"It sounds intelligent enough to me," he replied. He told me that the American Psychiatric Association publishes a manual of diagnosis, the *Diagnostic and Statistical Manual of Mental Disorders.* In it, mental illnesses are listed with code numbers that are used on medical insurance forms to collect premiums. Each coded mental illness has an official set of symptoms to form an accurate, "official" diagnosis. The psychiatrist must determine whether the patient exhibits the symptoms used to describe each of the official coded mental illnesses in the book.

"This guide is as precise as you can get," Barrett said.

"Regardless of what the book says," I told him, "I still believe my mother was suffering from a functional illness: paranoia. She was paranoid; then she suddenly became delusional. I've learned that delusions are a symptom of organicity. What I don't understand is how a functional illness like paranoia can suddenly transform itself into an illness that exhibits symptoms of organicity."

"There are five categories of organic brain syndrome," Barrett explained. "One of them, *dementia,* is often confused with *paranoia.* But in order to diagnose someone as a dementia patient, the hospital has to locate a 'specific organic factor,' which you tell me it hasn't done in your mother's case. That doesn't mean, however, that she doesn't have dementia. She may have it; we just can't prove that she does. She could have

paranoia and dementia, but without the 'specific organic factor' we could diagnose her only as paranoid.
Don't you see why it is best to treat her as if she is
suffering from both? Don't you think it's better to play
safe even if we can't prove that she has both?"

"How can you treat anybody for anything," I snapped,
"if you can't determine what precisely is wrong with
that person?"

"A correct diagnosis is essential to formulating a
course of treatment," said Barrett, "but let's face it: diagnosing a mental illness is not like diagnosing a physical
illness like tuberculosis or gout. Functional and organic
illnesses mimic each other and coexist. There are cases
in which one illness may express itself with the symptoms of another. Diagnosis is extremely tricky, and we
still know so little about the workings of the brain, we
may never really know what is precisely wrong with
your mother no matter what name we give her illness."

"What happens if Conrad is wrong?"

"If he can't come up with an adequate diagnosis,"
Barrett said, "nobody can."

13. During the next week, her third in the hospital, Esther's depression grew more intense.
She lay in her bed dozing or just staring into
space; her lips became dry and cracked. Enormously
weak, she had to be lifted up to be spoon-fed; occasionally she would call out for water, in a scratchy, enfee-
bled little voice and we would prop her up and help
her drink. After a small sip she would collapse back
onto the pillow, too weak to remain in an upright posi-

tion. Apparently her struggle with the bedpan had ceased and she appeared to have given up looking after her bodily functions altogether; the nurses continued to take their time cleaning up after her.

Her ankle also became swollen inside the heavy case. Often the leg injury sent pins-and-needles sensations up and down her body, which no one could do anything about. Esther was constantly uncomfortable, and occasionally in great pain. She was also kept in the restraining jacket around the clock and the fact that she had no freedom of movement alternately depressed and infuriated her.

"Maybe the family meetings will help," Sam told me hopefully. But then on Friday, three days before the first meeting, Conrad called and told Sam he felt that Esther was too depressed to participate and suggested postponing the meeting until the following week. It was hoped, he said, that she would be ready by then.

"What if she isn't?" Sam asked.

Conrad replied that they would just have to wait and see. He reminded Sam that with patients this age, these depressions could last a long time.

Each time we arrived at the hospital, we hoped this would be the day that Esther's depression began to lift. But as day after day went by with no change, we grew more and more depressed ourselves.

By now we were familiar faces to all the hospital staff, but they remained aloof when they saw us.

One day I walked into the lounge and encountered Rose, who was there on a fifteen-minute break. "The nurses are very cold," I said as I sat down beside her.

"That's the way they're trained in this unit. At first, they really get involved and go out of their way to please their patients. Then a patient will turn against them for no reason at all. Or he'll accuse them of things they didn't do. Then the nurses realize these patients are really sick and are just using them. Mental patients like to play games and they can't be trusted. The doctors and nurses learn how dangerous it is to become too friendly, too nice, with people like this. No matter what a patient says he needs, or how nice a patient pretends to be, they have to be professional and keep their distance."

"Do they really teach you that here?"

"They certainly do. They teach you that this place isn't a hotel, it's a mental ward, and these patients are very sick people. Many of them get worse no matter how you treat them. No one really knows how to help crazy people help themselves. Give them everything or give them nothing. If they're going to make it they're going to make it, no matter what you do or don't do. If they want to get better, they have got to do it for themselves."

Another week went by and Esther showed absolutely no improvement. Because of her ankle injury she was almost entirely immobile and was usually in great pain. The sweating of her ankle under the cast gave her an itch she could not reach. During most of her waking hours she was in constant torment. Conrad asked me to attend a meeting without Sam.

"Your mother's depression is getting worse and she still isn't ready to participate in a family meeting," he began. "We've decided that if it doesn't improve during the next week, we'd like your permission to use electroshock therapy."

I was appalled.

"You'll have to sign this permission form," said Miss Carr, the social worker.

I pushed it away. "I can't sign this," I said, "without

more information. I don't know a thing about electro-shock therapy. I don't know what it is. I don't know how it is used. Is it dangerous?"

Conrad sighed. He began to speak as if by rote. "Two plates are attached to the patient's head," he began. "Then a carefully controlled pulse of electricity is passed through the patient's head."

Miss Carr nodded in acknowledgment.

"There is an initial contraction, followed by a general-ized convulsion."

I winced.

The psychiatrist noted my negative reaction. "Your mother won't feel the convulsion. She'll be anesthetized and won't even remember the treatments. Besides, the convulsion is necessary for a therapeutic effect."

Once again Miss Carr nodded.

"Why is the convulsion necessary?" I asked.

"We don't really know. ECT has been used effectively for forty years and many theories have been advanced about its success. But there is no one acknowledged ex-planation. It's felt that perhaps the electricity in some way alters amine metabolism in the central nervous system, and those alterations have a beneficial effect on conditions like depression."

"It's a faster procedure than drugs," Miss Carr added. "It works with ninety percent of the patients; drugs work with only seventy percent. We've done it many times, with enormous success. It's really one of the pre-ferred methods of treatment."

"Your mother's an ideal case," continued Conrad. "People who have never had mental illness before have always been prime candidates. And ECT seems to work better with older people than with younger ones."

"Are there any side effects?" I asked.

"Headache. Some muscular pains. Some patients also

complain about memory loss. If we don't do more than three treatments a week, the memory loss usually lasts only about a week."

"How many treatments are you planning to do?"

"We can do as many as twelve or fifteen. I plan to do only four at first to see how it goes."

"Does the electricity damage the brain?"

"Some studies indicate that many, many treatments produce brain damage. But only if there is something organically wrong to begin with will the treatments make the damage worse. In cases like your mother's, which seem to be functional in nature, there is not much to worry about. Besides, we don't plan to give her that many treatments."

I looked searchingly at Conrad; then I looked at Miss Carr. "My mother seems to have *organic* brain syndrome, though the tests indicate that there is nothing organically wrong with her. Even you are treating her as if there is something organically wrong. Suppose there is. Then these treatments could make her worse, couldn't they?"

"It's an extremely small risk," said Conrad. "It's a chance I'd take if I were her son."

"It *is* an extremely small risk," echoed Miss Carr. "Definitely better than letting her lie there in a paralyzing depression."

I still did not know enough about electroshock therapy to make an intelligent decision. I also resented being pressured. I felt I should talk to Sam before I allowed myself to be persuaded. "I'm sorry," I said, "but for the moment electroshock therapy is out of the question."

Conrad seemed disappointed. "Miss Carr, you have something to discuss, don't you?" he said.

"If we're not going to try ECT, I think we should then discuss the necessity of a nursing home," Miss Carr began. "We bring this topic up with you first so that you can then take it up with your father. It's better sometimes to have a family member discuss this reality with an older family member than have it come from a member of the staff."

"The solution to my mother's problem surely can't be permanent commitment," I snapped.

"If your mother stays the way she is, there is no way she can go home."

"But we've got to assume she will get better," I said. "Isn't that what this hospitalization is all about—finding a way to help her get better?"

Miss Carr continued as if I had not interrupted. "Your father is not equipped to be a twenty-four-hour full-time nurse," she forged on. "Taking care of people who don't want to take care of themselves is an awful job. You've complained to the nurses about their performance. But you don't know the difficulty of taking care of one person, no less a floor full of patients like these. If your mother goes home, eventually your father and you will become worn down. In the long run, you will realize it is more humane to have her in a place that cares for her with no expectations about her recovery— even if you don't like the way they do their job. Isn't that better than having her at home surrounded by two exhausted, nervous people hovering over her, waiting for a breakthrough that may never ever happen?"

"A nursing home is out of the question."

"Think about it. Discuss it with your father, then we'll talk again."

"We'll talk again," Conrad repeated. He opened the office door.

I got up and made my way down the hall to Esther's room. She lay immobile in her bed.

"It's Henry," I said. I gave her hand a squeeze.

Esther said nothing.

"It's Henry," I repeated. I leaned over the bed. For an irrational moment I wanted to shake her and keep shaking her until I shook away the depression.

"They hate me," Esther muttered.

"Why?"

"They won't give me a bedpan. I need a bedpan."

"I'll get you a bedpan," I said. It was the only thing I could do.

I headed to the nurses' station.

"This is the third time we've changed her today," Mrs. Stanton said wearily. "You can't expect us to change her every half hour on the hour. You can't." She moved right past me and marched down the hall.

I stood in the doorway and watched as Mrs. Stanton entered the room. I looked at Esther and she was in terrible shape. I hated myself for thinking it, but maybe Conrad was right. Maybe she did need electroshock therapy; maybe with people this age, there was not much anybody could do.

I wanted to talk to some other expert. I wanted to hear some good news. I did not want to call Barrett again, so I called Esther's internist Dr. Nathan. I brought him up to date.

"Unfortunately psychiatric medications are not my specialty, so, sad to say, I'm inclined to trust them in this area because they're the experts," he told me. "If she can't be helped, I'm sorry," he added. "Very sorry indeed."

Sam and I sat together that night eating pizza. "What happened at the meeting?" he asked me.

Slowly and gently, I explained that the hospital had asked for our permission to give Esther electroshock treatments.

"That frightens me," he said. "What did you do?"

"I did not give my consent. It seems to me to be a

treatment of last resort, something you do when every-thing else fails."

Sam nodded. "What else happened?"

I took a deep breath and moved on to the next difficult subject. "The feeling is that if she doesn't get better, it may be too difficult for you to keep her at home. They feel that she might have to be sent to a nursing home."

Sam looked away. He spent a few minutes composing himself. "I can't believe this is happening to me," he said quietly. "None of this makes any sense to me."

"It doesn't make any sense to me either."

"I'm just confused and frightened." Sam looked at me imploringly. "Every family has its tragedies," he said quietly. "I know they come on suddenly and unex-pectedly. Every day people face crises like these. I made up my mind not to complain but to just do the best I can. But there are a few things I've got to get off my chest."

"What's up?"

"I have no one else in the world to talk to now. I've never been so alone. I just want to tell someone that it isn't fair for people who have always tried to be kind and decent to be struck down like this. I just don't know why this is happening to us. I've always tried to do the right thing. You've always tried to do the right thing. Esther has always tried to do the right thing. Is this our reward?"

I said nothing. I felt just as awful as he did.

"A year ago—six months ago—three months ago—did you think you'd be having this discussion about shock treatments and nursing homes? Doesn't it scare you?"

"Yes."

"I don't understand this illness. I don't understand the treatment. I don't understand the attitudes at the hospital. Does it make sense for her to be lying in that bed begging for help and all they can come up with is shock treatments and nursing homes? What do you really think of that hospital?"

"The hospital doesn't care about Esther the way you and I do," I replied. "They're doing the job they think should be done, the way they've been trained to do it."

"Do you think she can be helped at all?"

"I think we've got to set a time limit to how long she can lie in Chelsea Hospital. Then if she's no better, we have to find a doctor or a hospital or a treatment that can help her. I also think we do have to deal with the possibility that she might not get better."

"You know what?" said Sam. "Rather than a nursing home I want her home, and that's all there is to it. I want her home with me."

"You may need a full-time staff to help you," I said. "Medicare may not be of much help, either. I remember reading someplace that they usually do not pay for home care. It may take all the money you've got. And I won't always be there. There will be times when you'll have to go it alone."

"It's an experiment I've got to try," said Sam. "I've just got to try it."

"If that's what you want, then no matter how bad it may get, I'm with you," I said.

Then and there we made a pact with each other: no matter how bad Esther got, we would bring her home and do the best we could. No matter what, a nursing home was out of the question.

14. Sam and I read everything we could about electroshock therapy. Nothing we read convinced us to let the doctors experiment with it.

I also read everything I could find about mental illness in the elderly. The literature described how hard these illnesses were to diagnose accurately, how some could be controlled and reversed through the use of medication, and how others proved untreatable. The literature also pointed out that often progress could be extremely slow. Sam and I set a two-month deadline before we would have Esther reevaluated.

Meanwhile, four weeks had gone by and Esther had her large cast replaced with one that extended to just above the ankle. A slipper was placed over the cast, and Esther was helped up. For the first time in a month, she was able to stand upright.

Twice a day she was encouraged to walk down the hall. Taking cautious little steps, she would make her way around the floor.

We felt lucky because Esther had also become alert enough to participate in the first family meeting.

Sam and Dr. Conrad sat in Esther's room. Esther sat in a chair by the window. Occasionally she would break out in a sweat and Sam would reach over and wipe her brow.

"Once a week we are going to have an hour-long family meeting," Conrad told Esther. "The purpose of these meetings is to help the two of you to work out your difficulties."

Esther, her eyes glazed, stared into space.

"If we know what your problems are," the doctor continued, "we can find ways to make life easier and happier for you." He turned to Sam.

"Sam, if necessary, are you willing to change your behavior?"

"Yes."

Conrad turned to Esther. "Esther, what's bothering you?"

Esther looked ahead blankly and said nothing.

"Esther, what's bothering you?" Conrad repeated.

There was a long pause. "They don't give me a bedpan," she finally said.

"Is there anything else?"

Esther said nothing.

"Were you upset because Sam yelled at you?"

There was no comment.

"Did he get on your nerves after he retired?"

Esther shook her head.

"Did he wear you out?"

Again, Esther shook her head.

"Were you upset because you couldn't find a place to live? . . . Were you upset because you did not have enough money to do what you wanted to do?"

Esther slowly kept shaking her head.

Conrad met Sam's eyes. They both looked at Esther. Esther stared straight ahead. "I want to go back to bed," she said, and closed her eyes. In a moment she was asleep in her chair.

Conrad got up. "Thank you, Esther." He left the room, Sam following after him. "We'll try again next week."

Soon after, Sam returned to Esther's room. She had been moved back into bed. He looked down at her; she looked blankly back at him. Then he scooped her up in his arms and held her to him. "Please, please try," he said. "You've got to try."

"They don't give me a bedpan," she said softly.

Slowly Sam let her fall back onto the pillow. She closed her eyes and instantly she was asleep.

For the next week, Esther's behavior was unpredictable. Now she had moments of lucidity, but they did not last long. But she also continued to stay in her bed for long stretches of time, uninterested in anything that was going on, refusing to speak to anyone.

On one day she lost her temper and screamed at and scratched a nurse; on another she began to tremble uncontrollably—nothing anyone did could stop the palsy. After dinner one night she began to retch—and again, no one could stop the vomiting. Still another unexplained incident occurred at six one morning, when her blood pressure suddenly began to rise. She was given antihypertensive medication, but her blood pressure rose higher. She was given more medication; it did no good. An even greater dose could not lower her blood pressure, which got so high the nurses alerted the heart attack unit. Finally, however, it did begin to fall.

She also continued to wet the bed and a rash formed on her inner thighs. Most of all, she still complained incessantly about not being given a bedpan when she needed one.

Esther's illness coming on top of his retirement radically altered Sam's life. Outside of his sports, his main pleasures came from being with his wife and helping her whenever he could. Esther did not drive and Sam especially enjoyed taking her on outings with her friends. Now there was no one to take anywhere.

Because Sam had had so many jobs—teaching, coaching, running a community center—he had never been alone during the day. With Esther at home, he was never alone at night. Now essentially he was by himself most of the time. I saw him every day at the hospital and usually we had lunch before and dinner afterward, but this could not fill up the time of a man used to so much activity.

Sam reported that all their friends called regularly. Everyone was shocked by Esther's illness, but everyone was sure she was getting the best of care. They wanted to know what they could do to help. They invited Sam to dinner and asked him to visit. He was genuinely touched by the way he and Esther were loved.

For the first time in his life, he began to go to the movies in the afternoon. By accident he even wandered into an X-rated movie, his first—the title sounded innocent enough—and the theater, believe it or not, had a senior citizens' discount. The film was a comedy and Sam loved it. It was set in a hospital that manufactured sex organs which were form-fitted to the patients. The pornographic part came as they were tried out to see if they functioned properly.

Sam was fascinated. "I liked this hospital better than I like Chelsea," he told me over the phone. "I trusted them more."

We laughed.

"I've been having some bad nights," he continued. "I sit in front of the television and I'm alone. This is Esther's home. She made it beautiful and without her it doesn't mean anything to me. I have a drink or two and I still can't sleep. I get so upset I start crying and I can't stop. I think about her and the way she was— lying there all tied up, her foot in that cast and no one giving a damn about her, and I start to cry. I'm astonished to feel these tears on my cheeks, but still, I'm doing the best I can. I made you a promise, but I really made it to myself, not to complain. I also made a promise never to give up hope, and I won't."

Because seeing Esther at the hospital took so much time, Sam frequently slept over at my apartment in Manhattan. I had not been to his new apartment since the time I had helped Sam transport the cartons to Long Island.

On a Friday afternoon after our visit with Esther, Sam drove me to his new home. He opened the door and I stepped in and looked around. The entire joyous phantasmagoria of their old apartment had been splendidly recreated. The effect was breathtaking.

"Do you think she'll like it?" he asked with genuine concern.

"She'll be amazed," I replied. "I'm amazed."

"When she comes home, I want everything perfect. I don't want her disturbed by anything."

Everything was as bright and beautiful as it had ever been. I didn't say anything, but I knew that Sam and I were thinking the same thing: The only thing missing was Esther. We both felt her absence; suddenly we were overcome by sadness.

Sam went into the kitchen to make lunch. After lunch we took a walk. It was a lovely October afternoon and we wanted to see the autumn leaves. We went to a local restaurant for dinner. Then we saw *Burnt Offerings*, a perfectly awful movie about a haunted house, which we both enjoyed a lot. Back at the apartment, we talked some more; finally we were ready for bed.

Sam, however, could not sleep and we continued to talk after he turned out the light.

"We haven't spent a day like this in years," he said. "I had a wonderful time."

"So did I." There was a silence.

Out of the darkness, Sam said, "I don't think Esther is that bad."

"What do you mean?"

"I think we've allowed the staff to brainwash us. I know Esther a long time. I know her better than anybody, and I don't think she would complain as much as she does if she was being treated properly, no matter how much they blame her complaints on her mental condition. One of these days I'm going to spend the whole day at the hospital and find out exactly what those doctors and nurses do and don't do. And I'll make you a bet: I'll bet they don't look after her when she really needs it."

Sam drifted off and I thought he had fallen asleep at last. Then he said, "I'm glad we're friends. This is so much easier to go through with a friend."

15. Sam began to bring small groups of visitors to the hospital. These old friends would cluster around Esther's bed and Esther would acknowledge them. Then after a few minutes, she would say, "You have to go now," and she would roll over and pretend she was asleep.

But at the third family meeting, she finally began to talk.

What was she upset about? Conrad asked.

She was frightened that Sam and she would run out of money.

Was there anything else?

Moving to a new apartment scared her.

What else?

She was silent. Sam sensed she had begun to have difficulty following a rational line of thought.

"I've lost weight," she blurted out.

"Why have you lost weight?"

"I have cancer," she replied, "and there's nothing I can do about it. All I can do is lie in bed and wait." She suddenly stood up. "Sam won't change," she announced. "He goes around slamming doors. He'll never accept me."

Esther turned and limped out of the conference room. She headed back to her room and climbed into bed. Sam followed after her, but she refused to speak to him. She refused to speak to anybody.

On two consecutive visiting days, Sam got to the hospital early in the morning, determined to spend the whole day there. Whenever Esther saw him, she turned surly and suspicious. Believing he had come to spy on her, she kept telling him to go away. But Sam would not budge. He wanted to know exactly what went on all day.

Sam observed that when Esther rang her bell, no one would appear. When she called out for water or a bedpan, she was usually ignored.

"When was the last time you moved your bowels?" he asked her.

"Days ago."

"Why haven't you gone?"

"I'm too constipated."

"Did you tell anyone?"

"They don't believe me when I tell them."

"I believe you." He knew Esther was telling the truth.

Sam headed for the nurses' station. "My wife hasn't moved her bowels in days," he told Mrs. Stanton. Mrs. Stanton thumbed through some papers on her desk. Sam's temper began to rise. "Did you hear me?" he shouted. Mrs. Stanton did not reply.

He banged his hand down on the desk. "Now do you hear me?" he shouted even more loudly.

"Hospitals know when their patients move their bowels," Mrs. Stanton said coolly. "They keep charts."

"I know my wife better than you do and she's no liar."

"We've told you over and over that you can't believe everything your wife tells you." Mrs. Stanton stepped out of the office. Sam followed her. "You're supposed to help people," he roared. "Then why don't you? My wife hasn't moved her bowels in days and you sit there and do nothing and call her a liar. *You're* the liars."

The patients stuck their heads out of their doors as Sam charged past their rooms. "Why don't you help?" he shouted. "Why don't you want to help your patients?"

Mrs. Stanton stared at him.

"I won't leave this hospital until you help my wife," Sam announced.

Not until he got repeated assurances from Mrs. Stanton that she would deal with Esther's "constipation" would Sam depart.

That night, Esther awoke with a start. There was a jabbing pain in her abdomen. She let out a scream, followed by another, then another. Help was summoned. It was decided that she suffered from an impaction, the abnormal immobility of feces in the bowel. She was given an enema, which did hardly any good at all. Then she was given another, followed by a third.

"I told you so," said Sam when he learned of this. "They didn't give her a bedpan when she needed one. That's one reason why she wets the bed. And they didn't listen to her when she told them she was constipated. That's why she's in such pain now."

The next night Esther began to pass a series of thick, bright red, viscous clots of blood. The blood stained her nightgown and bedsheets. She touched herself, then stared down in horror at her hands. Stunned, she believed that her worst suspicions were true—she was in the hospital because she had cancer. The bleeding was the proof of it.

She grew even more depressed, and nothing anyone said could dispel the illusion that death was imminent.

The bleeding went on intermittently for a week.

"Look at my fingers," Esther said weakly. We stared at her bloodstained fingers.

Her condition was horrifying. "We've got to get her out of here," I suddenly said. I charged down the hall to Miss Carr's office and banged on the door.

The social worker opened the door a crack. "I'm in a meeting," she whispered when she saw me.

"I want to get my mother out of here," I shouted. "Now!"

She stepped outside. "She can leave whenever she wants to," she said evenly. "She voluntarily signed herself in; she can voluntarily sign herself out."

"Nothing here is helping her. Do you know that she's lying there *bleeding?* I don't care what your reputation is. I'm going to get my own doctors."

"If you notify us, you may bring any doctor you wish into the hospital. We welcome suggestions and advice. We'll do anything we can to help. The problem simply is that there is not much that can be done with patients like these. Problems like the one you're experiencing today are all too frequent."

"I'm tired of hearing that not much can be done," I snapped. "Damned tired."

I went to the pay phone in the hall and called Barrett to tell him what had happened. Then I asked him to come into the hospital and see for himself.

"I can't do that," he told me. "We have rules of professional conduct and it's just not professional to go into another hospital to check up on the staff. If you want me to come to the hospital to examine her, I will go only on the condition that I'm invited by your mother's doctor."

When I got home I began to call other doctors. I spoke to their secretaries, their answering machines, the doctors themselves, as I searched for a recommendation for an expert geriatric psychiatrist who would come into the hospital to give a second opinion about Esther's condition.

All the psychiatrists were cautious. They listened but usually refused to comment even though each made a speech explaining why his school of psychiatry—psychoanalysis, behaviorism, chemotherapy—was superior to the others. Each agreed to see Esther after she left the hospital. None, however, wanted to go into the hospital and examine her on my behalf unless personally invited by Conrad. They all seemed protective of each other; none wanted to be the one who might see something wrong and have to testify against a colleague in case there was a malpractice suit.

I made a list of hospitals and began to call them. Each was willing to take Esther, depending on the availability of a bed; none could give me any information about what could be done for her in addition to what had already been tried until they met and observed the patient. None would allow me to visit when I said I had to observe a hospital in action before I allowed my mother to become a patient.

I did not trust anybody any more. I also did not know what to do and I could find no one to turn to.

16.

An action taken by Conrad brought my search for help abruptly to an end. Esther had been in the hospital eight weeks and had just finished her fifth family meeting. She was always restless now and had trouble sitting still.

"I want to go back to bed," she said as she paced back and forth.

"Why?" asked Conrad.

"I'm tired."

"How would you like to go home?" he asked.

Esther eyed the doctor suspiciously.

"Would you like to have an afternoon pass?"

Sam had not known it was coming. He was amazed. So was Esther.

"When?" she asked nervously.

"The day after tomorrow. Your husband will pick you up at ten in the morning; he'll have you back in time for dinner."

Esther tried to smile. Sam could see that she was very tense. He reached out and took her hand. They sat there silently while Sam looked at Esther and Esther looked away. Slowly, the idea that she was going home for a day sank in. She turned toward Sam and smiled faintly.

That afternoon we sat in Conrad's office. "This is the schedule," he told us. "Take her home on Wednesday. If all goes well, we will give her a weekend pass and she'll go home for the weekend. A week after that, in ten days, she'll be discharged, on November eleventh. We will refer you to a local agency for medical and psychological help. We will also refer you to an agency so that you can hire a practical nurse. You will not be able to do this yourself. Do you understand that you are really going to need help?"

"Yes," Sam replied.

Conrad turned to me. "If you want to go along on Wednesday, fine. But I don't think you should be there on the weekend. This is an experiment for your father as much as it is for your mother. Mr. Katz has got to see if he can manage having her at home and you have to give him a chance to see what he can and can't do without help from the outside. Now, do you have any questions?"

"Why have you decided to discharge her?"

"There's nothing more we can do here. She's on a maintenance dosage of haloperidol, which will keep her psychotic symptoms under check. Now what she needs is time. With time, we'll see if she stays the same, improves, or gets worse. She might as well go home if she can. I'll be in my office when you get back. Knock on my door and tell me how it went."

Esther was dressed and waiting when Sam and I arrived on Wednesday morning. She wore the outfit in which she had been admitted. A nurse had helped her with her hair and had applied some makeup, but nothing could disguise the permanent glazed look that had been with her from the first day she had begun taking medication.

The guard unlocked the door. "Let's go," said Sam. He smiled cheerfully at Esther, but she stared straight ahead. He stood on one side of her, I on the other, and we led her through the doorway.

I waited with Esther in the lobby while Sam went to get the car. Esther looked around. "I like this lobby," she said. "It looks like a stage setting."

Sam pulled up and Esther got in the car, and very soon after the car began to move, she fell asleep, and did not wake up until the car stopped. Sam opened the car door for her, helped her from the car and led her up the stairs into the building.

He opened the apartment door and Esther stepped into her new apartment. All she needed was one look to realize that Sam had done a perfect job. She looked at her beloved collections, then she looked at Sam. Her eyes filled with tears as Sam led her to the dining room table. He was very proud and pleased.

We sat down and Sam made coffee. Esther's hands were shaking and there was a slight tremor in her neck. Occasionally she would get up and pace. Even though I knew that she might be restless, it hurt me to see her walking back and forth in this compulsive manner, unable to sit down for more than a few minutes at a time. Esther was apologetic about her inability to stay still and naturally we both reassured her. She wanted a drink and Sam gave her some ginger ale. I noticed that her lips were so dry they had cracked in several places. Sam and I tried to keep some sort of conversation going. Esther, however, who had always liked to hear the latest news about her friends, did not want to listen.

"I want to go for a walk," she said.

We were all so edgy that we welcomed an opportunity to get out of the house, even though we'd been there for less than a half hour.

Sam led us through the shopping district, but Esther, who had always loved to browse, was not interested in any of the store windows; she had to keep moving. But she also tired easily. Endlessly on the move, she was simultaneously exhausted by her restlessness. Nevertheless, she could not stop.

"I'm hungry," she said.

We walked quickly to the nearest restaurant. Esther looked at the menu. Her eyes went up and down the page, but she registered nothing. She had not been able to concentrate on print from the day she had been admitted to the hospital.

"I want the turkey dinner."

While we waited for the food, Esther got up and began to pace. People stared at her, then whispered to each other. Sam stood up and was about to get her when I stopped him.

"Let her walk," I said quietly. "It's impossible for her to sit still."

When the food arrived, Esther took her place. She picked up her knife and fork. Her hands trembled so much that she was unable to cut her food. Sam took her plate and cut it for her.

Esther bolted down a few pieces of turkey and then resumed her pacing. She roamed around the restaurant and then returned to the table. She ate one or two more pieces, then pushed the plate away with most of the food untouched. She was done. She did, however, order a huge piece of whipped cream cake, which she gobbled down.

We returned to the apartment and sat for a few minutes. Esther paced some more.

"Well, I think it's time to be going," she said suddenly. She was afraid of losing control, afraid of her restlessness, afraid of the freedom, afraid that she would be judged, afraid that she wasn't doing well enough. She wanted to be back in a controlled environment.

Sam was dismayed. "But we don't have to go back to the hospital until four o'clock."

"I still think it's time to be going."

"I think we should do what Mother wants," I said.

As on the trip home, there was no conversation in the car. When we got Esther to her room, she seemed relieved—almost happy to be there.

Dr. Conrad appeared on the floor. We had returned early enough to catch his round. "You're back early," he observed. "How did it go?"

"She has no concentration," Sam said. "She can't sit still. How is she going to stay in the house if she's so restless?"

"You'll have to learn to work with it. It's one of the symptoms of her problem and it may diminish in time. Once you get help, you'll be able to leave her and you won't feel so trapped by her restlessness."

Sam frowned. He did not want help. He did not want to leave her. What he wanted was for Esther to be better.

"I still think she should go home for the weekend," Conrad added. "Then we'll finalize the discharge date."

"All right," said Sam. "Anything you say."

Conrad smiled at us. "I'd like to thank the two of you."

"Why?" I asked, surprised by his sudden friendliness.

"The families of many of the patients Mrs. Katz's age use the hospital as a dumping ground," he explained. "I know you've been upset with the hospital, but we would rather have you concerned and upset with us than like the others, who find these patients so difficult they're glad to be rid of them."

"I can't believe families would just leave their relatives here and let them rot," said Sam.

"I can't tell you how many do," replied Conrad. "They just can't cope with people this troubled. There's almost nothing as burdensome as an elderly patient who is mentally ill. It's a burden many families do not want to bear."

That night, I got a call from Esther. "I had a very nice weekend at my house," she said.

"But you haven't spent the weekend there yet. It's only

Wednesday night. The weekend doesn't start until the day after tomorrow."

"I went. I'm not going!"

"What's the matter?" I asked.

"I'm scared."

"What are you scared about?"

"There's something wrong with me and nobody can do anything to help me," she replied. "I'm scared because I'm sick and I'm getting sicker and I know I can't be helped."

"You're doing fine," I said.

"Don't lie to me," Esther replied. "I know I'm a lost cause."

17. Sam called me early Saturday evening to tell me that Esther's weekend at home was following the pattern of her afternoon visit. "She's restless and needs constant diversion," he reported. "But she has no interest in anything. She can't even stand the sound of the radio or television. She stays in her bed for hours. She eats very little but craves sweets. The palsy and the constipation are still there and she's always thirsty."

Determined to make Esther comfortable, he jumped right in and dealt with all of it. He was afraid that if she was displeased she would grow even more difficult; he dreaded the possibility that she would become so difficult he could not take care of her at all.

When Esther returned to the hospital she went to bed immediately. The strain of a weekend at home had been too much for her. She sank into a depression that was deeper, uglier and more impenetrable than any she had had before. Unable to articulate or even acknowledge what bothered her, she responded to nothing any of us tried to do to restore her. The discharge scheduled to occur that week was postponed.

A week went by and all she could do was thrash around in bed, lost in despair. One day as Sam sat by her bedside, she sat up suddenly. "You're trying to get rid of me," she snapped.

"You know that's not true."

"You don't love me, you just don't."

"That's not true," Sam said again.

"Get out," Esther said suddenly. "I don't want anyone near me who's trying to get rid of me."

"Esther . . ."

"Get out!"

She became so agitated that Sam did as he was asked.

At the end of that afternoon, Esther appeared at the nurses' station. She stood there tentatively. Tears streamed down her cheeks.

"What can I do for you?" asked Rose.

"I'm upset."

"Why?" Rose asked.

"Because I didn't tell my husband the truth."

"What did you tell him?"

Esther recounted the morning's conversation.

"Why don't you call him up and apologize?"

Rose led Esther to the pay phone where they waited their turn. Esther's hands were so shaky she could not deposit the money.

Rose did it for her and dialed the number. Then she handed Esther the receiver.

"It's Esther," Esther said when she heard Sam's voice. "I'm sorry."

"That's okay," Sam replied.

"I was wrong when I said you didn't want me around. I know that wasn't true. Okay?"

"Okay," said Sam.

"I'm going to go now."

"Fine," Sam said. Then he added, "I love you."

"I love you too."

"I'm glad you're coming home."

"So am I." Esther hung up and turned to Rose. "He loves me," she told the girl.

Four days later she was discharged.

18. When Esther got home and was settled, I felt free to make a quick trip to California. From Los Angeles, I kept in touch with Sam, talking to him as often as four times a day.

He reported that he had to help wash, dress and bathe Esther. The slightest difficulty would overwhelm her and she would take to her bed. The nervousness had not improved; neither had the palsy or the constipation, and Sam was forced to hire a visiting nurse to come every other day to administer an enema to her.

Sam had been told that the physical symptoms would persist and he was prepared to deal with them, but he was put under a great deal of unanticipated stress by Esther's continual repetition of the same conversation: that she would never be well. He could not bear to think there was nothing he could do to make her feel happier.

Thanksgiving came soon after Esther had been discharged. I took a long weekend and flew home for the holiday. It had always been our favorite family holiday and this year there was plenty to celebrate, Sam told me. Esther was home and she *would* get better. He decided to take us all out and made a reservation at a restaurant.

On Thanksgiving Day, however, he seemed edgy when he took my coat. "I've changed my mind. I think we should eat in. It will be easier." I knew Esther was not in good shape.

She came out of the bedroom. "I can't button my blouse," she said. "My fingers are too stiff. I can't reach back there." She began to pace. "I can't dress myself. How can I stay home when I can't dress myself?" Esther looked straight ahead. Her eyes were blank. She stood rigidly erect.

Sam began to set the table.

"I'm not right. I just am not right."

The palsy was worse and tremors had now afflicted Esther's entire body. I took her hand. It was so stiff I thought a finger could break off in my hand.

"I'll get the food now," Sam announced.

"I can't eat. I'm not right."

"Henry will stay with you and I'll be right back." Sam threw on his coat and hurried out the door to buy our take-out Thanksgiving dinner.

Esther and I sat at the dining room table. "I'm not right. I'm not right," she said again.

"It takes time."

"No. I'm getting worse. I know I'm getting worse."

"You're not getting worse. If you were getting worse, they wouldn't have let you come home."

"They couldn't do anything for me. I can't be helped."
"Nonsense."

Esther leaned over and stared into my eyes. "What am I going to do if Daddy dies?"

"I'll take care of you," I said gently.

"Daddy doesn't want me," she replied. "He wants to put me in a nursing home."

"What makes you say that?"

"I heard him on the phone. The two of you are planning to put me away. You don't want me anymore."

"That's not true." I realized that Esther had overheard a phone discussion Sam and I had had about taking her to the Institute of Living in Hartford, Connecticut, an institution I had recently read about in a newsmagazine. She had confused this treatment facility with a nursing home.

She sat down beside me and took my hands.

"I'm sorry I'm so sick. I didn't want to be 'mental.' I can't help being 'mental.' "

"You're going to be fine."

"I'm not right," she repeated again. "I'm just not right."

Esther jumped up and resumed pacing, taking speedy little jerky steps as she navigated the same circle over and over again. "What's going to happen to me?" she asked as she rounded each bend. "What's going to happen?"

I sat there watching her. I knew she couldn't stop her pacing; I knew she couldn't feel any less anxious than she did; I knew there was nothing I could do to help her at the moment. I also knew something had to be done soon. None of us could go on like this.

Finally, Sam returned. He went into the kitchen and unpacked a large shopping bag filled with aluminum food containers. Determined to make everything look attractive, he opened the containers and put the food on serving platters. These he placed on the table, which he had set with their best china and prettiest linen napkins. First he served Esther and then he did the same for me. Last of all he helped himself.

Esther picked up her knife and fork. Her hands were shaking. She began to eat. Then she put down her knife and fork. "What will happen to me if you die?" she asked.

Sam did not reply but kept on eating.

"I'm not right," Esther said again.

"It's Thanksgiving," Sam pleaded, "and we're together. Isn't that wonderful? We're together. Try to eat your dinner."

"You want to put me away. The two of you want to put me away."

Esther got up from the table and stood in front of us. She was growing more agitated. "What's going to happen to me if Sam dies?" she asked again.

"I'll be here. I'll look after you," I said again.

"You're both going to put me away."

"I promise you that you will never be put away," I repeated.

"What's going to become of me?"

"Will it make it easier if we go over what will become of you?"

"Yes."

I turned to Sam. "Can we?"

We stopped eating. Sam went into the bedroom and returned with a boxful of papers. He spread them out across the table.

We sat there solemnly, the three of us, contemplating the possibility of my father's death.

Sam gave me a piece of paper and a pencil, and I began to take notes. "Here is a life insurance policy," he said. He read off the number and I wrote it down. "To collect the money, all you have to do is fill out an application and file a copy of the death certificate."

"Who will do that?" asked Esther.

"You and Henry will."

"What happens if Henry isn't here?"

"I'll be here. If anything happens to Daddy, of course I'll be here."

"I can't sign my name. My hands shake too much."

"You can sign your name," I said, as I gave her a pen and a piece of paper. Slowly, letter by letter, she did.

Sam went on. He explained his will, his cemetery deed, his small portfolio of stock, his social security benefits and his retirement plan. He then explained how to have his funeral costs paid for.

Esther looked at me. "I want you to promise me," she said, "that if something happens to Daddy, you won't put me back in that place. You'll take care of me."

"I promise."

Esther got up and paced, while Sam methodically picked up his papers and put them back into his box.

"You see what it's been like," he said to me before he returned the box to the bedroom.

Esther stood over me. "It won't be easy," she said. "I can't dress myself. I can't button my clothes in the back. I can't remember anything. I'm just not right." She extended her hands. "Look at my hands. Why do my hands shake so much? What's wrong with me?"

We stared at her hands. They fluttered before her as if they had a life of their own.

19. Chelsea's psychiatrists had instructed Sam to contact the Maple Hill Mental Health Center if he had any problems. The center was an agency on Long Island affiliated with Maple Hill Hospital in New York City, a distinguished medical institution near Gramercy Park. The Monday after Thanksgiving Sam telephoned the center. He spoke to a counselor about Esther and made an appointment for a social worker to visit their apartment. Esther insisted that she was too ill to have any visitors, but Sam realized that if it were left to Esther, no one would ever visit them again.

On the day that the social worker was to visit, Sam went out and bought a beautiful cake from the best local bakery; he cleaned the house and made little sandwiches. He wanted the meeting to go well because he hoped that a successful visit would encourage Esther not to be so afraid of the outside world.

The meeting did go splendidly. The social worker, Francine Pink, was a radiant young woman. Esther and Sam liked her from the moment they laid eyes on her.

Francine spoke gently to Esther. She watched her pace back and forth; she observed the fixed stare and the tremors. She urged Sam to take Esther to see Dr. Benjamin Sudhalter, who was the director of the center and a senior member of Maple Hill Hospital's psychiatric staff. "He's a very wise and compassionate man," she said earnestly, "and I've seen him reach out to people who were so isolated that it seemed no one could reach them. There may be a short wait, but I'm going to try to have him see her as quickly as possible."

She also urged Sam to attempt to get out on his own a bit more and suggested that if he did not want to leave Esther alone, he take her to the Maple Valley Center, where there were a number of classes for senior citizens.

Sam persuaded Esther to take Francine's advice about the center and Esther decided to study gardening. She was one of four women in the gardening class. First the students were taught how to plant a tomato plant.

Esther picked up the trowel. It shook in her hands. She was embarrassed. The teacher tried to help her hold it, but it was impossible and Esther dropped it in frustration.

The women had been asked to bring in their dead plants to discuss what they had done wrong. Esther had no interest in dead plants. She paced back and forth during the discussion. By the time the class was over, she had decided not to go back.

Francine next suggested they attend Riverview Hospital's day care center for the elderly. At the hospital, they had lunch, participated in a group sing-along and were entertained by a clown.

Sam felt foolish. He didn't want to sing along with anybody; he didn't want to watch a clown. He couldn't wait to make his escape. However, he had to admit to himself that Esther did seem to enjoy the clown's magic tricks and she had been able to sit still for the show.

A few days later, Francine called to tell Sam that Dr. Sudhalter would meet with them at the end of the week. Sam got up early on the morning of the meeting and helped Esther dress. Convinced that Esther was slipping, he was very nervous about what Dr. Sudhalter might tell him about her condition and dreaded that this new doctor would insist that Esther was not well enough to remain at home.

My father had called me in Los Angeles as soon as he learned of the appointment. I got a few days off from the *Sgt. Pepper* preproduction and flew in for the meeting.

I immediately liked Sudhalter. A man of great warmth, unlike Dr. Conrad, he went out of his way not to be patronizing. He also spoke clear, concise English.

He asked to see Esther alone. Francine joined us and did her best to deal with Sam's nervousness while we waited for the doctor to call us in. Finally Sudhalter asked us to join him in his office.

"How is she?" Sam asked.

"I'm not right," Esther said. "I'm just not right."

"You may not be as bad as you think," Sudhalter told her. He turned to Sam. "Your wife's symptoms are not caused by mental illness."

"I don't understand."

"Your wife is suffering from an overdose of haloperidol. This overdose of medication has given her Parkinsonism."

We all listened intently. "You are suffering from Parkinsonism," Sudhalter told Esther. "The medication you are taking is the cause of the tremor in your hands, the staring, the rigidity, the restlessness, which are all symptoms of Parkinsonism. The medication has dilated your pupils—that's why you can't read; at the same time it has sharpened your hearing—that's why you can't stand the sound of the television. Too much haloperidol can also cause irritability and depression. A medication like this may have a number of other serious side effects: drowsiness, lethargy, nausea, vomiting, rapid heart rate, constipation. When did the symptoms begin?"

"Esther became depressed a week or ten days after she began taking the drug. Her hands began to shake a month ago," Sam responded.

"Didn't the hospital experiment with the medication to see if the depression would go away and the shaking disappear?"

"No," said Esther.

Sudhalter shook his head in disbelief. "Are you telling me that this depression has been going on for three months?

"Do you remember any discussion about changing

the medication to an antidepressant after she became depressed?"

"They said they couldn't because of Esther's high blood pressure."

"Are you sure they said that? There are some occasions when antidepressants can even *lower* blood pressure."

"We weren't told that," said Sam. "We were told that Esther could never take antidepressant medication."

"I can't think of a better place to experiment with medications like these than in a hospital," said Sudhalter.

Once again he shook his head. "Lastly," he said, "I'd like to know if you experienced any of the other side effects I mentioned."

Sam told the doctor about all the peculiar physical symptoms that Esther had acquired while she was hospitalized. He also spoke of Esther's constipation and the complications that had ensued.

"Didn't they give her a stool softener?" asked Sudhalter. "Psychiatric medication is extremely constipating." After the first two days of constipation, you always give a stool softener. If the constipation persists, then you have to start giving regular enemas as long as the patient stays on the medication.

"They didn't believe Esther when she told them she was constipated," said Sam. "They didn't believe her until she was in pain."

Sam then described how Esther broke her ankle the first day she was at Chelsea.

Sudhalter repeated what Dr. Nathan had already told me, that an older patient on a large dose of a drug should always be carefully watched. Since she had been a wanderer, he wondered why she hadn't been restrained. Why hadn't a nurse been posted at her door?

"I don't want to have Parkinson's disease," said Esther. "Will it go away if I stop taking this medicine?"

"You don't have to have Parkinsonism. You don't have to be depressed. I've got to get your records from Chelsea to find out if there were specific medical reasons for giving you this medication instead of any other. If you do have to take this medicine, as a last resort I can prescribe antiParkinsonism medication. I've also got to find out why your medication wasn't changed after you became depressed. I must have these answers and I must have them quickly."

"Is there hope for me?" asked Esther.

"There's plenty of hope, but first I've got to see your records. Meanwhile I'm going to slowly reduce the dosage of haloperidol you are taking. I have a hunch you'll do just fine."

"I can't believe there's hope for me," Esther said as we headed for the car.

"There is hope," said Sam, the smile on his face reflecting his joy at the news he had just received.

"You won't tremble," I said. "You won't stare. You'll be able to read. You'll be able to watch television."

"Why did this happen to me?" asked Esther.

"None of us understands why any of this has happened," said Sam. "But we do know that you're going to get better. I think we should celebrate."

"I agree," I said. Esther began to cry. "You should be laughing," said Sam. "We should all be laughing. Follow me."

He took us to a fancy French restaurant for a victory lunch. By the time lunch was over we all felt wonderful.

That afternoon Sudhalter called Chelsea Hospital to ask for Esther's records. He also made the request in writing.

A week went by. The records did not come. Another week went by. I, too, called and wrote to Chelsea, explaining the situation. Yet another week went by without a response. All of us began to call Dr. Conrad and Miss Carr, neither of whom returned our calls. I also wrote a stern letter to the hospital superintendent.

The records did not come. Dr. Sudhalter continued to reduce Esther's medication but he repeated that he needed to study the records before he made any drastic changes in her treatment plan.

I had no alternative. I went to Chelsea Hospital, marched into the records office and began to shout. Like my father, once I got started I could not stop, and just as the hospital had attempted to pacify him, they sought to pacify me, telling me the job would be done immediately.

Another week went by and there still were no records. My lawyer advised me to write to the county medical society.

20. While Dr. Sudhalter waited for the records, he continued to have regular visits with Esther. Anxious to discover the cause of her illness, he questioned her about her medical history. Sam reported that he asked if she had ever been told that she had had a series of small strokes.

"No," Esther had replied. "Why do you ask?"

"Small strokes sometimes deprive the brain of just enough oxygen to cause conditions like this," the doctor had told her.

"It makes sense to me," she had replied. "It explains

why my hands shake. It explains why I've suffered memory loss. I bet I did have a series of small strokes."

From that moment on, she would occasionally attribute her illness to a "small" stroke.

Finally, the records arrived, forty-one anguished days after Sudhalter first wrote for them. Despite what we had been told about Esther's illness being functional, Esther had been given an official diagnosis of one of the organic brain syndromes, dementia. Though there was no evidence of it, the records reported that this diagnosis was nonetheless the consensus of the treating physicians. The records also reported that antidepressant medications "were probably contraindicated because of the presence of organic heart disease," and so none had been prescribed.

The records stated that Esther had been referred to a clinic on Long Island for "family sessions" and to have her medication monitored, and that "family therapy in this case would be extremely valuable along with low-dose haloperidol medication."

Obviously "family seminars" and "low-dose haloperidol medication" had not been the answers to Esther's problems, thought Sudhalter.

He had a hunch. He didn't care that the "consensus of the treating psychiatrists" at Chelsea Hospital thought that Esther was suffering from an organic brain syndrome. Often the symptoms of a depressive disorder are confused with those of dementia. In order to determine whether Esther was in reality suffering from depression and not dementia, he would have to take away all of her medication. He would then be able to observe the symptoms of mental illness that still persisted. He called us all to a meeting.

"I have read the records," he told Esther, "and I would like you to stop taking haloperidol immediately."

"What should she take?" asked Sam.

"Nothing."

Sam looked shocked. "Nothing?"

"We've got to see what's really wrong with you before we can figure out the proper medication," he explained to Esther. "Once we take you off everything, we'll have a fair idea of the problems we're dealing with."

Sam was terrified. No one knew what it had been like to be Esther's custodian when she had sneaked out of the house and run through the streets pleading for help. He did not want to go through that again. On the other hand, Dr. Sudhalter believed that Esther's restlessness and depression were caused by the drug. So Sam agreed to remove Esther from all haloperidol.

For the first three days without the medication, Esther remained unchanged. Over the next five she began to recover some of her old energy and spirit. We dared to hope that as the haloperidol left her system, Esther would be well.

Two weeks later, the symptoms of Parkinsonism were all gone, but the depression had returned and the delusions seemed to be returning. Also when Esther began to wake up in the middle of the night and call out because she believed there was a stranger in the room, we became increasingly nervous. It appeared now that unless positive action was taken, major problems were inevitable.

Sudhalter decided that Esther could be helped only if she was readmitted to a hospital. In a controlled environment, he would have the chance to test his hypothesis: that she was suffering from depression, not from dementia. In a hospital, he could safely experiment with the antidepressant medication he believed would help her. He knew how hard it would be for us to send Esther to another hospital, and he called Sam and me to ask us to meet with him.

When Dr. Sudhalter told us that he wanted to put Esther back in the hospital, our initial reaction was skepticism. To prove his point, he took out Esther's records and went over them with us. He explained that depression was often mistaken for dementia. "I think it is essential that your mother be treated for depression and not dementia," he said emphatically. "In the hospital, we'll start her on extremely low doses of an antidepressant. No matter what these records say, and no matter what you've been told about the dangerous interaction of antidepressant medication and high blood pressure medication, I'm convinced Esther can safely take the antidepressants. In the hospital we'll watch her blood pressure carefully anyway, just to make sure there are no problems. She should be taking these medications in a controlled environment, where oxygen, life-saving devices and nurses are all available. I want her in the hospital because I want her safe."

Sudhalter looked at me. "You look very troubled," he observed. "What's bothering you?"

"A doctor once told me that dementia was often mistaken for paranoia. Now you're telling me that depression is often mistaken for dementia. How do you expect me to trust any of you?"

"Often it is informed guesswork," Sudhalter continued. "But I believe this guesswork is better than throwing up your hands and doing nothing."

"I can't help feeling guilty about everything that's happened. I don't want to feel guilty anymore. I don't want to make another mistake. I'm not a stupid person," I continued, "but I didn't understand a thing about this illness when it began. So I believed everything I was told by Esther's doctors. When I was told about electroshock treatments and nursing homes, I assumed that's what doctors tell you when a patient cannot be helped. Between my own prejudices about this illness and what I was led to believe at the hospital I had become convinced that my mother's illness was almost irreversible. I could never have believed then that the medication she was taking was making her worse."

"Most people are trained to trust doctors and hospitals automatically. Unfortunately, many doctors do believe that as people get older, they can't be helped. The only intelligent way to deal with these illnesses—which are happening to more and more people each day—is to make sure that every internist who treats older people is versed in the mental illnesses that accompany aging. Few do know anything about these diseases. That's one reason why so many older people are subjected to bad medicine in this area.

"I don't want to lecture you and I know you're very concerned, but what happened was a case of the wrong thing at the wrong time and not a series of evil acts directed specifically toward you.

"The evil is in a system that encourages psychiatrists to believe that the elderly can't be helped. It's a question of attitude as much as anything else. You've got to believe that older people *can* be helped. If you don't, you'll never be able to do a thing for them.

"Chelsea Hospital is a teaching hospital that trains doctors to be psychoanalysts. Residents in their psychiatric ward who are training to be psychoanalysts often have little exposure to geriatric patients. The resident who treated your mother is not an unintelligent or insensitive young man and he's not stupid either. He went to medical school and now he's a resident at a good hospital. I'm sure he would have liked to do a remarkable job. But unfortunately he is under a system that trains him psychoanalytically. Psychoanalysis is a technique that usually is not helpful in dealing with older patients. This resident is being trained to treat articulate, middle-class people who can sit or lie still for forty-five minutes two or three times a week for a five- or ten-year treatment period.

"What happens when an elderly patient arrives who can't sit still for ten minutes, let alone five or ten years? That hospital isn't interested in patients like this. Nor does it take much interest in drug therapy. The psychiatrists at hospitals like Chelsea usually don't thoroughly understand psychiatric medications, much the way a doctor versed in chemotherapy might not thoroughly understand psychoanalysis.

"Such doctors should never accept a patient like Mrs. Katz; they should take only patients with whom they can do a job. But in psychoanalysis, the analyst is trained to play the role of God: He is always right, he never makes mistakes. Since these doctors are trained to believe that they are always right, they go ahead anyway and discover they can't do much good. So what do they do then? They recommend a nursing home. A substantial percentage of all the mental patients in nursing homes don't need to be there, but they're buried there anyway."

He shrugged resignedly, then told us that he believed that the psychiatric profession in general has never liked the elderly anyway. He explained that approximately twenty-five percent of the nation's elderly suffer from mental illness, but the National Institute of Mental Health directs only about four percent of its resources for services and research into the mental ailments peculiar to older people. "As far as psychiatry is concerned, the elderly are a profit-making institution," he announced. "It's not fashionable to think of them as curable even though so many are; it is fashionable to put them away and make money off them by testing them, evaluating them, counseling and charging their families for them until they die."

Sam and I were stunned.

"I was totally trusting when my mother was in the hands of Chelsea's psychiatrists," I finally said. "Now I may never trust another doctor or hospital again."

"That's perfectly understandable," said Sudhalter. "You made mistakes, yes, but many people do far worse than you did. Somehow, you have steered your mother to a place where she might be helped. There are many relatives of the mentally ill who never get that far." He smiled consolingly. "Let me tell you about the psychiatric ward at our hospital," he continued. "Your mother will be in a unit run according to the principles of milieu therapy. Milieu therapy simply is a manipulation of the hospital environment to make the patients help each other get better. All the patients and staff members in Esther's unit are considered part of a therapeutic community. The members of this community meet to deal not only with problems of individual members of the community, but also with problems of the entire group, and everyone is encouraged to take responsibility for everyone else. We believe you can't solve people's problems by spending an hour or two a week with them. So we turn all the patients into therapists and have the therapy go on full time. This wasn't done on your mother's floor at Chelsea, but it's a technique that is practiced on mental patients elsewhere.

"I think she'll do well at Maple Hill."

I told Robert Stigwood that I wanted to remain in New York for the duration of my mother's hospitalization. He told me to take all the time I needed.

I went to Long Island to tell Sam that I was staying

in New York. Sam looked troubled when I saw him.

"I don't like the idea of hospitalization," he told me. "I'm afraid more harm may come to her. Yet I can't think of anything else to do."

"What I've learned is to trust you," I replied. "You *do* know mother better than anyone. When it comes to my mother, I trust you more than any doctor. If you think something is wrong, I'll act immediately—and I won't ask any questions.

"We'll visit her every day. We'll find out the name of every drug she's given and make sure we know the side effects of each one."

"We'll watch them every single minute of the day," added Sam, "and the minute we smell something suspicious, we'll take her home immediately. We will be like watchdogs."

"We'll never make the mistakes we've made before."

"No, we won't, but still I hate it," he said. "I hate her being in the hospital. I hate me being here alone. I hate not knowing if anything will do any good at all. This isn't like the first time," he continued. "I'm not naive anymore. I don't automatically expect good treatment from anyone."

Neither of us said anything. Apprehensive about what the future would bring, we were both doing our best not to surrender to that apprehension.

"I can only hope that the hospital will help," Sam finally said. "If it doesn't, I'm prepared to bring Esther home immediately. And I'll tell you something else," he added. "I know that until we find something that *does* help, neither of us will give up."

21. On the morning we were to leave for Maple Hill Hospital, Esther decided she did not want to go.

"The last hospital didn't help me," she pleaded. "It made me worse. How do you know this hospital won't hurt me too?"

We went over the reasons that she had to be hospitalized again, but it was no use.

"Why must I go? I don't shake anymore. My foot is barely healed. I could bleed internally again."

I did not know what to do. "You have to go—just for a few days. It's breaking all our hearts to send you, but you've got to go." I picked up Esther's bags and walked to the front door.

Esther began to cry. "You both want to put me away. That's really the truth of it. This is really your way of finally getting rid of me."

Sam fought back his own tears as I opened the front door. Once inside the car, Esther stared straight ahead. She refused to look at either Sam or me. Sam backed out of his parking space and pulled away.

The admission procedure at Maple Hill's psychiatric unit was accomplished with ease. The paperwork had already been done and the admitting officer merely introduced herself and directed us to the proper floor.

We got out of the elevator and when I saw the locked steel door, I was sure the ward at Maple Hill Hospital would be just like the one at Chelsea. I was really surprised by how different it was. For starters, the noise and energy were startling. Some patients were walking about the main corridor, some were sitting around a portable radio, while another, on a low bench, played guitar, as others sat around him singing along. It was a boulevard at high noon with everyone out for a stroll.

Chelsea's mental ward had been mostly old and white

and female, with a few psychotic teen-agers, and no middle range. In this ward there was a great deal more diversity. There were people of all ages and all races with plenty of nurses and doctors moving easily among the patients.

An orderly took us to Esther's room, a "semiprivate," which in New York parlance meant it had four beds. Two of the beds appeared to be occupied, though no one was in the room. The orderly put Esther's suitcase on a rack at the foot of one of the unoccupied beds. Esther was told she would meet her roommates later. She began to toss her things into a bureau drawer.

Sam had not slept well for the past few nights. Guilty and distraught about leaving Esther, he now began to act in a not-quite-rational way. It was as if he imagined that if he left Esther with some external order, it would be magically transformed into internal order and she would be well. Sam removed the rumpled clothes from the drawer, folding and arranging them neatly.

"I think we should go," I told him. "Mother can unpack herself."

Esther looked out of the room. She took in the hippie guitar player, a tough-looking fifteen-year-old black girl, an older boy with blond streaks blended through his hair.

She stepped back into the room. "I don't want to stay here."

"We've got to go," I repeated to Sam.

Sam turned and shouted at me: "I'm just trying to do things right." Then he went back to his compulsive folding.

"We'll have a real problem if you don't get moving."

"I'm not staying here." Esther began to pull from the drawer all the things Sam had put in it.

"Let's go *now*," I said.

Suddenly Sam caught on. He turned to go.

"I'm not staying, I'm not staying," Esther called out as she followed us down the hall. "Please take me home."

A buzzer went off and suddenly Esther was caught up in a group of patients lining up to receive their medication.

We got to the door and the guard opened it. "I want to come with you," Esther shouted.

"We will see you tomorrow," I said. "You'll be out of here before you know it."

Sam turned to Esther. "We'll be here tomorrow."

"I don't want to stay here." Esther reached after us. But the guard held her back. She had begun to cry again. "Take me home, take me home," she pleaded as the guard pulled the door shut after us.

Sam and I were numb. "It gets rougher," Sam said quietly. "No matter what we do, it gets rougher."

We sat in the office of Dr. Morris Ball, who was the supervisor of Esther's unit.

"Dr. Sudhalter has gone over the case with me," he told us. "First we're going to try an antidepressant, amitriptyline. The drug—if it works—will gradually improve mood as well as relieve depression."

"How does the drug work?" I asked.

"Without involving you in a long, technical explanation about chemical precepts, it is believed that the drug slowly restores to normal levels certain constituents of brain tissues that transmit nerve impulses. Basically the drug has been successful in relieving the symptoms from which your mother suffers. Frequently, when we relieve these symptoms, the mind can heal itself."

Sam and I were surprised by this information.

"It may take a week or two or three before we see any change at all, so let's all relax and meet once a week to bring each other up to date."

Whenever I visited Esther during the first week of her stay, she seemed a little less agitated but not any more communicative. I noticed that in the second week, her mood had begun to lift. Nothing prepared me, however, for the phone call I received from Sam at the end of that week.

"She's her old self!" he exclaimed joyfully. "She's cheerful. She's put on makeup, she's had her hair done. She's not pacing. She's reading. She remembers things! We've got Esther back!"

"I don't believe it."

"See for yourself."

I rushed to Maple Hill. When I arrived, Esther was calmly sitting in a chair in her room, reading a magazine. Sam sat beside her, smiling happily.

"Hello, darling," Esther said when she saw me. She kissed my cheek.

I sat down on the bed and stared at her. For a moment I thought I might be dreaming. Had this all been one horrible hallucination? "How are you?" I asked.

"Absolutely fine," she replied. "This is such a lovely hospital. I've met such interesting people here. They have such interesting stories. Wait until you meet them. I want you to meet all my new friends."

"I'd love to," I replied. I was astounded by her control.

"How's your movie?" she continued. "When are you leaving for L.A.?"

"At the end of the month."

Esther beamed. "I'm so proud of you. It's so exciting. She reached out and gave me a hug.

I still was not sure if I was awake or dreaming.

Dr. Ball stood in the doorway, watching us. He caught my eye and smiled. "What do you think?" he asked.

"It's wonderful," I said.

"A favorable response to antidepressant medication can be swift and dramatic," he told me.

"Do you really think I'm doing well?" Esther asked him.

"You certainly are."

"I feel as if I've had amnesia," she said. "I remember a little about my floor at Chelsea Hospital. Then I remember going home and I remember coming here. I don't remember what happened before I went to Chelsea Hospital and a lot of what happened there. It's as if a year of my life has been erased."

"That's understandable," Ball said gently. "I've explained to you that not being able to remember recent events is a symptom of your illness. As you continue to improve, so will your memory."

"It's still a little strange. I've talked to the people here. They're used to having whole portions of their lives erased. They don't remember six months of their life; then one day they wake up feeling fine, never knowing if they'll lose another six months sometime in the future. I find it puzzling. Don't you?"

"It can be," Ball said quietly.

"I know that there have been some people who thought I was going to become a vegetable."

"A vegetable?"

"A person who can't take care of herself. I knew somehow that I would never become a vegetable. I also knew that my son knew and my husband had faith in me. It's good to know that the people you love believe in you."

Ball nodded his head in agreement. "You will never be a vegetable, Esther."

Esther extended her hand. Sam and I got up and Sam helped her to her feet. "Let's go for a walk. I want you to meet my new friends."

Arm in arm, the three of us walked from the room into the hall. It was an amazing moment, one that I found almost impossible to believe. I had my mother back!

22.

Esther was now capable of socializing and she plunged into the life of the unit. Sam and I watched her and enjoyed the pleasure she took in making friends with the other patients and hospital staff.

"I love my roommates," she told us.

I got to know them and I liked them too. They were named Marilyn and Nell. Marilyn was an unkempt teen-ager who was phobic and delusional; Nell was a mousy woman in her mid-twenties who was both anorexic and depressed.

Marilyn always looked messy and straggly. She would rarely eat and was almost always cold. She wore layers of sweaters and made her family bring extra blankets from home so she would not shiver at night. She was barely nineteen and had been in and out of mental hospitals from the time she had been a small girl. None had helped. Everywhere she went, she felt cold, tired and afraid.

Marilyn was also a talker. She talked. And talked. And talked. Nonstop. None of the patients wanted to be buttonholed and they all ducked when they saw her coming.

Esther told me that she thought it was improper to ignore Marilyn. And I observed that she would be the only one to sit and listen attentively whenever Marilyn approached her.

"When I get out of here, I bet I can be like anyone else," Marilyn would begin. "I could get a job. I bet I could. I could even have my own apartment. Who knows? I might even get a boyfriend. My parents have always discouraged me. But even if they discourage me some more, I bet I can do it. I can be like everybody else. I can get a job."

When Marilyn would stop for a breath, Esther would speak up. "If I was young now, I would have made up my mind about what I wanted to do," she would tell Marilyn. "I would have gone to school to be an interior decorator because I love to think about colors and forms and furnishings. But when I was young, girls didn't think about anything but getting married. You're still young and you're luckier than I was. You're growing up in a more informed world. You've got a chance to do something special with yourself."

Marilyn thought for a while and then said, "Whenever I talk to you, I always feel better."

Esther said thoughtfully, "I think that it's important to have a dream. You've got a good dream. You just have to make sure no one discourages you."

"What are your dreams?" asked Marilyn.

"I'm too old for major dreams," Esther replied. "I just want to go home and be with my husband."

Esther's other roommate, Nell, had tremors not unlike those that Esther had had. Many of the other patients teased her cruelly.

Esther, with memories of her own Parkinsonism fresh in her mind, refused to join in. "Nell is amazing," she told me.

"Why?" I asked.

"She's smaller than anyone else. She's thinner. She's sicker. And she keeps going."

Everywhere she went Esther called Nell amazing, and by the time she was done Nell was dubbed the "Miracle Patient." It was a name that stuck to her throughout her hospitalization.

A few days after Esther made her dramatic recovery, I learned that the empty bed in Esther's room was assigned to a new patient, Karen, who related to me the story of her first meeting with Esther.

None of the women was in the room when Karen checked in. Esther was the first to return. She found Karen lying on her bed, sobbing. Esther sat at the edge of the bed and looked down at Karen. "Do you want to have a snack?" she asked. "A snack always makes me feel better."

Karen shook her head.

"My name is Esther. What's yours?"

"Karen."

"You shouldn't be so upset," said Esther. "This is really a very nice hospital. There are plenty of activities and meetings and parties. I'm busier here than I've ever been in my whole life."

Karen was still crying. "This is the fifth time I've been hospitalized," she sobbed, "and none of the hospitals helped me. There's something in me that makes me want to kill myself. Maybe I should kill myself now and be done with it. I've tried three times and failed each and every time. I can't even do that right."

"I'm here," said Esther, "because of my memory. I can't remember the name of the President of the United States." Esther shrugged her shoulders. "Whoever heard of a country that locks you up because you can't remember the President of the United States?"

Karen could not help laughing. Esther laughed too. She took Karen's hand. "Let's have that snack."

Dr. Sudhalter had explained that psychiatrists at Maple Hill Hospital practiced milieu therapy; but I had no idea how busy this therapy would keep Esther. She participated in three meetings a week devoted to discussing the patients' psychological problems. At these meetings, everyone—both patients and staff—was encouraged to submit opinions and recommendations. There was also a fourth weekly community meeting, during which the unit would deal with the social problems of the patients—those who were disruptive, those who were in the habit of borrowing but not returning, those who gossiped about the other patients. Esther was also in a smaller group that met twice a week for group therapy.

The patients and the staff lunched together every Tuesday afternoon. On Friday evenings, patients and staff would see movies selected by committee representatives. Every Sunday afternoon, the ward would give a party. The patients would decide what refreshments to serve and then they would shop for them. They would do all the decorating. Families and friends of the patients were invited to these festivities, which were usually highlighted by folk singing and social dancing.

There was further interaction. Occupational and recreational therapy groups abounded and patients on different floors could participate in the senior citizens' group, a play-reading group, and a crafts group.

The staff worked hard to reinforce the patients' positive behavior. I thought back to Esther's floor at Chelsea, where Esther's attempts to control her own body received no support from the staff, where, when she said she was constipated everyone thought she was lying.

Unlike the unit at Chelsea, where Esther was isolated in a room by herself, it was made clear to the patients that they were to reinforce each other's positive behavior, just as the staff did. Roommates were encouraged to become friends and to share their experiences with each other.

Once a week, I met with Dr. Ball and Dr. Sudhalter. Since Esther was doing so well, our conversations were brief, friendly ones.

"Esther is still upset about her memory loss," Sudhalter told me at our first meeting after Esther's recovery, "and nothing we can do can convince her that it's temporary. I suppose she'll just have to wait and see for herself."

"Will all of her memory come back?" I asked.

"There's no reason why not," Sudhalter replied. "There's no reason why everything won't be fine."

Though Sam and I explained to Esther that her memory would return, she maintained that this was the reason she was being kept in the hospital. Neither Sam, nor I, nor the doctors could do anything to dissuade her.

Entering Esther's room one afternoon, I overheard her addressing her roommates: "I'm afraid they won't let me go home unless I can learn my new phone number and address, and I can't seem to remember a thing."

"We'll help," Karen said immediately, as Marilyn and Nell nodded agreement.

They decided to write out the answers to certain vital questions. Esther would study them and then they would question her until she knew the answers by heart.

Esther spent the day studying. The next morning they started the questioning.

From that moment on, she was expected to know the answers no matter where she was or what she was doing. She would be heading for the television room, when Nell would call out: "Hey, Esther, who's the President of the United States?" She would be on the medication line, when Karen would walk past her, turn and say: "Esther, what's your address?" All day long for a week, she was quizzed incessantly.

Finally, at five in the afternoon on Friday, all primed and ready, she went to see Dr. Ball for her weekly conversation. When she returned she was crestfallen.

"What happened?" asked Karen.

"The minute I walked into his office I forgot everything," Esther said sadly. "When he asked me what day of the week it was, I confused yesterday with today." She shook her head. "Think of the situation. I may never go home unless I can remember the name of the President of the United States."

"I don't think that's likely," said Karen.

"Dr. Ball also got upset when I told him I still had trouble dressing myself. They may not let me go home unless I get strong enough to fasten my brassiere."

Everyone laughed.

"Don't laugh. That's the way it is. In this world, they think you're sane if you can remember the name of the President and you're crazy if you don't. What a peculiar world!"

"What is the name of the President of the United States of America?" asked Karen.

Esther thought and thought. "Ford!" she finally exclaimed.

The women shook their heads.

"Nixon?"

"No."

Esther was exasperated. "Tell me his name," she said wearily.

"Jimmy Carter."

"And if I remember that, I'm sane!"

The women laughed again.

Esther brimmed over with indignation. She had never tried to kill herself; she didn't think she was Jesus Christ; she had never been a member of an all-girl gang in the Bronx; she had never seen a Quaalude. "I just can't remember the name of the President of the United States and I'm too weak to fasten my brassiere. For that they want to give me life!"

She stared down at her hands, which still were weak from the Parkinsonism. She hated her physical weaknesses as much as her loss of memory, and was determined to regain her strength as well as learn the answers to the questions she considered silly. The occupational therapist had given her a ball to squeeze and she squeezed it ferociously as she roamed the halls, saying over and over again: "The President of the United States is Jimmy Carter."

But when put to the test, she still forgot his name. Huge chunks of her memory were gone, and though she joked about it, and wouldn't admit it to anyone, she was deeply frightened by her memory loss.

23.

Esther even tamed Benson, the most difficult patient on the floor. A wild-eyed, long-haired young man in his early twenties, Benson—his fellow patients never called him by his first name—played his guitar continuously and chanted endless unrhymed songs of his own creation. He had delusions that he was a great rock-and-roll star and all the other stars called him because he had the best songs, the best band, the best dope and the best women. Benson was diagnosed as "manic depressive." When he was depressive, he was suicidal; when manic, he was aggressive to the point of violence, stating that only an audience with Bob Dylan could cure him.

Benson would provoke arguments that inevitably led to fistfights. Wisely, most of the patients steered clear of him, the women especially hating him because he would make lewd suggestions and try to paw them whenever he got the chance.

Esther liked Benson's singing and guitar playing. She thought that if he wanted to meet Bob Dylan he should meet Bob Dylan. She did believe that Benson's language and aggressiveness stood in the way of his success with women, but she was convinced he would "grow out of it." There was nothing terrible that one couldn't grow out of if one set one's mind to it.

"Benson," she said, "there's something you should know."

"What is it?"

"My son is a rock music critic. He's interviewed the Rolling Stones and Led Zeppelin and Elton John. He even got his cousin an autographed picture of Rod Stewart."

"The Rolling Stones are shit," Benson snarled, "and Led Zeppelin sucks. I'm better than all of them put together."

"What do I know?" Esther replied. "The only one I like is Alice Cooper and that's because he dresses like a chicken."

"I'm better than Alice Cooper."

"You should play for my son. He knows a lot of important people."

Benson was suspicious. "Would he listen to me?"

"How could he turn down a mother who's 'mental'?"

Benson did not reply. He marched into his room, slamming the door behind him. Esther could hear him singing and playing his guitar behind the door. She knew the seed had been planted.

She told Karen about what she had done.

"Watch out for him," Karen replied. "Mrs. Jackson, the head night nurse, told me his whole story. He's been in and out of fights since he was five. He bashed in a kid's head with a lead pipe when he was twelve and he's been a ward of the courts ever since. He's filled with medication and he's still violent. Do me a favor. Keep your distance."

Esther got up and headed for the pay phone.

I listened to the whole story. "Have you heard him sing?" I asked.

"Yes."

"Well?"

"It's not quite the *Hit Parade*... but it has potential."

"I see."

"He just needs someone to pay attention to him. That's what he needs. You will encourage him, won't you?"

"Of course," I replied, promising to appear at the hospital at the end of the week.

Benson rehearsed night and day. His songs dealt with interplanetary wars, crime on the subway, a life of celibacy contrasted with a life of lust, and the problems you go through if your name is Jesus Christ. Each was at least twenty minutes long.

At the appointed time, I arrived at Maple Hill. Smiling happily when she saw me, Esther marched down the hall and fetched Benson, who had cleaned up for the occasion. He wore pressed jeans and an unspotted T-shirt. His hair was washed and combed and he was freshly shaved. He approached me nervously and we shook hands.

Benson took out his guitar and began to sing. The

patients gathered around, listening and then glancing at me to see my reaction. Meanwhile Benson sang on. Two songs were terrible; one wasn't.

"He's doing very well," Esther whispered to me, at the end of the third number.

Finally, it was over. Benson glared at me.

I started to speak, but Esther jumped right in and gave me the cue. "You'll help him, won't you?" she asked me.

"I certainly will."

"He'll help you!" Esther exclaimed. "That's all we have to hear. Benson, you've done well. It's reason for you to get well and get out of here."

Esther turned to me. "What will you do?"

"Benson," I said, "when you get well and do get out of here, I will take you and a tape of your songs to someone at a record company who can give you some professional advice. That will be a real beginning for you, but it will only happen if you get yourself well."

"Do you mean it?"

"I mean it."

Everyone broke into applause.

"Snack time," Esther announced suddenly. "The strain of all this has made me hungry." She marched out of the dayroom, the other patients following her.

Esther stood in front of the refrigerator. In a minute she had organized an assembly line; I watched as she efficiently supervised the making of a dozen cream cheese and jelly sandwiches.

"In occupational therapy yesterday," she told me, "they said that I might want to consider becoming a short-order cook."

After dinner, many of the patients watched the evening news. Then they would follow Esther into her room.

Esther, who enjoyed being outspoken, would give her views about what they had just seen.

I received Dr. Ball's permission to join them one night for this after-dinner ritual. President Carter had been in office a short time, and every move he made was the top story of the day. Esther could not remember his name, but that didn't stop her from having opinions and speaking out.

"Once Sam and I stayed in a motel in Rocky Point, North Carolina," she recalled. "As I was checking in, the owner of the motel looked at me and said, 'You sure do use a lot of makeup, ma'am.' Then and there, I could see that this man didn't know how to run a motel. A motel owner either treats his customers respectfully or he minds his own business. This man didn't exercise common sense. By being disrespectful, he demonstrated that he suffered from 'narrow brain.' I don't know anything about Jimmy Carter—I can't even remember his name—but somehow he reminds me of that motel owner. For the next four years I hope he won't be saying, 'You sure do use a lot of makeup, ma'am,' to all the wrong people."

Esther then turned to the winter weather and the fact that the fierce cold wave had not deterred a record number of car robberies.

"Do you know about all the land upstate that isn't being used?" she asked rhetorically. "That land should be turned into camps where young people are taught a trade. If hundreds were trained and paid, for example, to clear up the snow as soon as it falls from the sky, then they wouldn't have to steal cars for a living, would they?"

She thought the draft resisters still in Canada should be brought home, "but don't tell the Ku Klux Klan I sent for them."

Esther opened a box of candy and began to pass it around the room. "I think we need a woman President," she continued. "A woman understands the problems of poverty and old people. Men do not."

The women applauded.

The decriminalization of marijuana? "If it's good enough to use in hospitals, it's good enough to use at home."

That got the biggest applause of all.

There had been a feature about aging on the news that night. "How do you feel about growing old?" someone called out.

"Terrible."

"Why?"

"Because old people are easy to push around. We've got to learn to take care of ourselves." Then she realized how serious she had suddenly become. "I'm just not accepting my age very graciously."

She then tried to name the President of the United States of America, the date, her new address and her new phone number, and struck out on every one.

"At this rate," she said ruefully, "I'm going to be answering your questions for a long, long time."

There was a broom closet at the end of the hall. At eight each morning, the cleaning woman would open it, take out the cleaning supplies and spend the next two hours cleaning the floor. The closet would remain open and unsupervised these two hours each morning.

One morning, Marilyn and Benson sneaked into the closet and closed the door behind them. A nurse walking down the hall was stopped dead in her tracks by the enthusiastic noises emanating from behind the door. She opened it immediately and Benson and Marilyn were reported to Dr. Ball.

The following morning, a community meeting was called and the staff and patients gathered to discuss what had occurred. The female patients were indignant. Convinced that the psychiatric medications they were taking had decreased their sex drives, they were offended by a meeting dealing with sex between patients when this topic now had such little relevance to their lives.

Sam and I sat in the dayroom with Esther and a group of friends who had come to visit. Esther described the meeting to us.

She then pointed out Marilyn, who was looking neat and clean. "She's even started to eat," Esther said. Next she pointed out Benson who was all spruced up.

Esther squeezed Sam's hand. "Now that they've gone into the closet together, they're both doing fine."

Everyone laughed. Her friends were glad to see her and she was delighted to see them. They all agreed that she was doing well. The noise and energy as well as the wild array of patients had originally bewildered them. But when they observed Esther's progress, their fears had vanished.

"On my floor at Chelsea," she continued, "nobody could think about going into a closet. Everybody was too depressed to get out of bed."

24. Maple Hill's psychiatrists had discovered that some ex-patients missed the drama and closeness of life at Maple Hill. Finding the outside world far less responsive, intense and concerned, they tended to become depressed after discharge. So the hospital had initiated a transition procedure. Before patients were dismissed, they received a number of weekend passes. Most important, they were transferred to private rooms when their discharge was imminent. Here they could learn to be alone again and not be afraid of their own company.

Early one morning, Dr. Sudhalter came on the floor to give Esther the news that she would be moving to a private room that day.

Esther did not like the idea, but she understood Sudhalter's reasoning and did not question it. She went back to her room and broke the news to her roommates.

Esther was feeling sad. She packed in silence. Her roommates helped her carry her possessions. Before they left her alone, they reassured her that the fact that she had her own room was proof she was making progress.

"I'm having trouble getting used to it," said Esther.

"We'll stay here until you fall asleep," Karen told her.

Esther got into the bed. Karen and Marilyn and Nell sat around the bed. They talked until Esther was drowsy. Only when they were convinced she could fall asleep, did they say good night.

25. "It's been an absolute miracle," I told Dr. Ball.

"I'd like to take credit for working a miracle," Dr. Ball replied, "but we just practiced basic medicine. We made a correct diagnosis and then properly administered the correct medication. As you've seen, these are extremely powerful chemicals. But they are administered by human beings and are only as effective as the people who administer them."

"Was depression originally the cause of my mother's illness?"

"It's conceivable that her depression expressed itself as paranoia. Your father retires. They have problems adjusting to retirement and your mother becomes unhappy and feels guilty about her unhappiness. In the minds of many people, the next stage after retirement is death. They realize they are part of the human chain and the fear of death, of illness, of loss of a mate, adds to the stress they already feel, triggering an insidious kind of depression that can express itself in a number of unusual ways, including paranoia."

"I can't get it out of my head that my mother broke her ankle the first night she was at Chelsea. That she was given a medication that gave her Parkinsonism instead of one that could help her. That she had trouble with the bedpan and with her bowels. That I was urged to give her shock treatments, told about nursing homes."

"A vendetta isn't the answer," said Ball. "After all, it's extremely difficult to make a malpractice suit stick against a psychiatrist. The courts tend to mistrust the testimony of mental patients simply because they are mental patients. You'll also need expert testimony. Many of the psychiatrists in this city know each other. They serve on committees together; they attend conventions together. They're members of a guild, and like medieval guild members, they're loyal to each other. A doctor won't testify against another doctor because he doesn't want another doctor to testify against him."

"That hospital was recommended to me by everybody.

I've also read about it from time to time. I thought it would have the best psychiatric services."

"Everyone assumes that if a hospital is well known it can cure all patients no matter what their problem.

"Unfortunately, it's a matter of luck. Your mother might have had amazing success in another hospital's psychiatric ward.

"Anyway, she's fine now. If I were you, I'd take her home and forget about it. Three of the patients with whom she became friendly—Benson, Marilyn, and Karen—have attempted suicide many times. They've been in and out of hospitals their whole lives. Your mother's going home; they're not. You've got cause for celebration. Now I don't want to discuss this anymore. Take your mother and go home."

I got up and went to look for Esther. Sam told me she was in her old room, saying goodbye. We waited and she came out into the hallway with Karen and Nell; Marilyn had been transferred to a sanitarium a few days earlier.

"You'll be out soon enough," Esther was saying. "Then you'll come to the new apartment and Sam will take us out to lunch."

"I may never get out," said Karen.

"You'll get out. If I can remember my address, you can do anything."

"You are the real Miracle Patient," said Nell.

They hugged and kissed and promised to be in touch.

"I'm a worrier," said Esther. "I want everyone to get well. I want everyone to help each other get well. Every night before I go to sleep, I'm going to think about you. Will I have to worry?"

"No," said Karen.

"No," said Nell.

"Will we have to worry about you?" asked Karen.

Esther shrugged her shoulders. "I hope not. But if you do, we'll all be roommates once again and we'll have another terrific time."

Esther then took Benson under the arm and began to walk the hall with him. "Pick up the phone and call me," she said.

"Yes, Aunt Esther."

"You'll let me know the minute you are released."

"Yes."

"You'll come over and I'll make you dinner."

"Yes."

"And don't forget about making the tape for Henry."

"I won't forget."

She kissed Benson on the cheek and Benson kissed her back.

She walked into the dayroom and waved goodbye.

"Speech! Speech!" called the patients.

"I had a very good time," Esther said enthusiastically. "Of the many, many hospitals I've been in, this one is my all-time favorite."

We carried Esther's belongings to the door. It was unlocked for her. She was smiling, but there were tears on her cheeks as she headed toward the elevator.

26. The minute we got Esther home, she pleaded fatigue and went immediately to bed. I had lunch with Sam. When I left Esther was still asleep. When she woke up, she told him she was still tired. She stayed up for a while, then fell asleep again.

Esther spent as much time as possible in bed. When

she emerged, any difficulty at all would necessitate her return. Her chronic exhaustion confused and upset her. She had been well for almost a month; why was she suddenly sick again? She was afraid she was suffering a relapse; maybe she really was incurable.

Sam's and my jubilation turned to dismay.

After her discharge from Chelsea, we had mistaken her severe Parkinsonism for mental illness; now we thought her extreme fatigue was a different symptom of the same illness. We called Dr. Sudhalter. He asked us to come in the next day.

"I didn't warn you about this," he told Esther, "because I didn't know whether it would happen. Some patients do well in hospitals where there are other patients on medication. The nervous systems of these patients have been chemically altered in the same ways: these patients are in 'synch' and can easily relate to and interact with each other. At home, however, you are the only person in your world taking medication. Your internal rhythms now are different from Sam's and Henry's. Being on a different rhythm with everyone is exhausting. And it takes a great deal of time to adjust—sometimes months."

Dr. Sudhalter assured us that eventually Esther would come out of it. He gave Sam the phone number of a local agency from which we could obtain a practical nurse so that there would be someone around to help Esther wash and dress, and be with her when he wanted to go out on his own.

After the meeting, Esther and Sam urged me to go back to Los Angeles. There was nothing I could do, Sam said; there was nothing more anybody could do.

"I'll be fine," said Esther. "I've just got to have the patience to wait until I'm back in synch with the rest of the world."

Even though Sam and Esther now understood the cause of her weakness and fatigue, Sam once again had to play the role of full-time nurse. Every day he would tell me he planned to get away for a few hours—to play tennis or golf—but he never went. Phoning from Los Angeles, I pleaded with him to hire someone. At first he resisted. He wanted things done right for Esther and he believed that only he could do them. But at last he realized that since Esther had come home, he had not had one single moment for himself and wouldn't unless he did get help. He promised to hire a practical nurse.

Worrying about whether her energy would ever return had made Esther tense. "I don't want a nurse," she told me over the phone. "I don't want anybody in white wandering about. It reminds me of a hospital." Then she stopped. "I guess you're right," she said. "Sam has been at my side every minute since it started. It isn't fair."

Sam took out the phone number Dr. Sudhalter had given him. Esther stood in the doorway as he called the agency.

The South Shore Home Care Service had commercials on local Long Island radio stations which said it specialized in offering help to those who were trapped at home with the "bedridden."

"I'm not bedridden," Esther fretted as he dialed the number of the service. "I'm just weak."

Over the phone Sam described Esther's condition to the agency representative. He was told that the agency would search for a nurse who was experienced with patients such as Esther and that they would call Sam back.

The next day the agency representative told Sam that he had assigned a woman named Minna Gordy to the case. Although the house was near the train station, Sam arranged to meet Mrs. Gordy at the station the following morning at nine in order to show her the way to the apartment. He was to look for a small black woman dressed in a nurse's uniform.

Esther was still asleep when Sam left. At the station, he spotted Mrs. Gordy at once. Gray-haired and tiny, she was an elderly wisp of a woman. Sam had not expected anyone this old or this frail.

Mrs. Gordy was exceedingly formal and polite. Her voice was very soft, almost a whisper; she also had a slight wheeze. She looked to be in worse health than Esther and Sam was concerned that she would find her new job too taxing.

As they walked home, Sam tried to make conversation, but Mrs. Gordy was very quiet. In the apartment, he stared at her. There was nothing for her to do until Esther got up.

"Would you like a cup of coffee?" he asked

"No, sir," replied the nurse. "What can I get you?"

"Nothing. Nothing at all. I'm fine."

They sat looking at each other, making small talk laced by huge pauses.

Finally, Esther came out of the bedroom.

Sam introduced them and Mrs. Gordy rose slowly to shake Esther's hand. Esther could feel the creak in Mrs. Gordy's arthritic legs.

"Don't get up," she said.

"I don't mind. What can I get you, Mrs. Katz?"

Esther's heart instantly went out to Mrs. Gordy. If she didn't need the money, Esther thought, she'd be home in bed too.

Esther turned to Sam. "Did you get Mrs. Gordy a cup of tea or something to eat? What would you like, Mrs. Gordy?"

Sam jumped up. "I offered her some food, but she said she didn't want anything."

"Of course she wants something. Get her something."

"I can make all of us something," said Mrs. Gordy. She headed slowly for the kitchen.

"Sam!" Esther exclaimed. "Don't let her."

"What can I do? I can't stop her."

Mrs. Gordy did her best to wait on Sam and Esther. Sam did his best to wait on Esther and Mrs. Gordy. Esther did her best to get Sam to wait on Mrs. Gordy. Convinced that her nurse needed nursing, she also did her best to make Mrs. Gordy feel happy and comfortable.

As the two women got to know each other, they became confidantes. They talked about their childhoods, their dreams and their symptoms. Both were anxious and fearful about the future. Because they really liked each other, each did her best to be brave for the other. They got along fine.

Esther learned that Mrs. Gordy had been born in Alabama and had married John Gordy, a plasterer, when she was just eighteen. The Gordys had migrated north and Mrs. Gordy had learned practical nursing, which she had practiced for almost thirty years. They had two sons, both of whom had made the army their career. For the present, one was stationed in Alaska and one in West Germany.

Ten years ago Mr. Gordy had died and Mrs. Gordy's nephew Jim and his wife, Sally, had asked her to move in with them. She would take care of their two young children and help with the house in exchange for living there. For seven years everyone had lived very happily together. Mrs. Gordy was like a mother to Sally, whose own parents had died long ago. And she was the only grandmother the children had ever known. Three years ago, however, Jim had died of a heart attack, although he was vigorous young man.

After Jim's death, Sally had asked Mrs. Gordy to stay. "This doesn't change anything between us," she had told her.

A year later, Sally had married again and in another year there was a new baby.

Sally's new husband was named Willy and he was the source of Mrs. Gordy's misery. Willy was jealous of the first marriage and especially of Mrs. Gordy. He was jealous of the little she ate, the little space she took, the little electricity she used.

Sally could not stand up to Willy and Mrs. Gordy now felt like an intruder in the house that had felt like home to her from the day of her husband's death.

Sixty-three years old, Mrs. Gordy suffered from an enlarged heart as well as arthritis. Nevertheless, she had gone back to work in order to earn enough money to move away from Willy.

Mrs. Gordy explained to Esther that her great solace was her role as an elder in the Long Island Star of Zion Baptist Church. The congregation consisted of one hundred and fifty families who prayed for each other, fed each other, comforted each other, and spent almost all their free time together. The church elders also taught Bible classes and Sunday school classes.

The center of all of this activity was their minister, Dr. Solomon Smith, a really wonderful example of pastoral concern. Dr. Smith made sure any member of his congregation who became sick was taken care of, and he had set up a small fund for those who were out of work; he had organized classes in the church to help people improve their reading and mathematical skills; he had established a day care center at the church for the many working mothers.

In addition to his pastoral skills he was a compelling preacher; his small church was packed every Sunday.

Even people who were not believers would come to admire his oratorical fireworks. After the morning service, the congregation had dinner together. By the end of the day, everyone felt well fed, cleansed of sin, and ready to set out and do good during the forthcoming week.

Esther asked Mrs. Gordy why she had never discussed her family problems with Dr. Smith.

"Everybody's got troubles, Mrs. Katz," she replied. "Most of the other people's troubles are much worse than mine. I do the work of the Lord by helping, not by being a burden."

"Then what are you going to do?" asked Esther.

"Help myself," Mrs. Gordy had said. "And you'll help me, I'm sure, and I'm sure the Lord will too."

Every day before she left, Mrs. Gordy told Esther that she would pray for Esther's recovery, and every day she did.

"I think hiring Mrs. Gordy was a wonderful idea. She's such a lovely lady," Esther told Sam.

"I like her too," Sam replied. He shrugged his shoulders. It was true that he was now able to get out by himself, but somehow he now had two patients instead of one.

A pattern emerged. Sam would get up at seven in the morning, wash, dress, and fix breakfast for himself. Mrs. Gordy would arrive at nine and Sam would leave. At ten, Mrs. Gordy would wake Esther—who still spent more than half the day in bed—and help her wash, dress and eat. By eleven-thirty the two women would be ready to venture out.

Walking wasn't easy for either of them. Because she

spent so much time in bed, Esther was weak and had little endurance. Mrs. Gordy had shortness of breath and arthritic pain. Leaning against each other, the women would walk arm in arm. Taking tiny steps and pausing frequently they would glance at one another to make sure each had the strength to go on.

Finally, they would reach the local park, where they would plop down on a bench—exhausted by the walk and at the same time gleeful and amazed that they had made it.

"You will get better, Mrs. Katz, I just know it," Mrs. Gordy would say as she caught her breath.

"How do you know it?" Esther would automatically ask.

"Because the Lord is looking over you, Mrs. Katz. He'll see to it that you do just fine."

"And if life gets too tough for you," Esther would then tell Mrs. Gordy, "you will always have a place to live. You can always live with us."

"Mrs. Katz, you don't have the room."

"If we have to, we will get a larger apartment and then you can move in. By then I'll be well. I'll be able to look after you."

They smiled at each other. When they were together, each felt more courageous and hopeful.

At the end of the hour they would walk home; by then Sam would have prepared a light lunch. They would eat together and then Mrs. Gordy would leave at two.

At first the walks were short and the women spent most of the time talking. Eventually the walks became longer before they treated themselves to a chat. Sometimes they were joined by a former patient of Mrs. Gordy's, a retired furrier named Phil Samuelson. Mr. Samuelson had cancer. He would appear in a wheelchair propelled by his grown son Nat. Mr. Samuelson was a friendly, talkative man who liked to travel beside them as they headed for the shopping district.

Mrs. Gordy had been Mr. Samuelson's nurse until he was taken to the hospital, presumably to die. But he had had a surprising turnaround and had gone home more fit than he had been in a long time. He was the local miracle and the women were always delighted to see him. They were also apprehensive.

"I'm afraid it'll come back," Esther would whisper to Mrs. Gordy.

"He's a goner," Mrs. Gordy would agree. Tears would fill their eyes.

When they did not see him for a day, they were sure he was sick again and the thought of it would make them weep. Then he would miraculously appear the next day, to their immense relief. Sometimes he'd miss two or three days, and convinced that he was dying, they would become desolate; then he would reappear and all would be well once again.

Esther and Mrs. Gordy had now incorporated window-shopping into their walking ritual. They also discovered the ice cream parlor, with its luscious hot fudge sundaes, the pizza parlor and the delicatessen. Esther would order and Mrs. Gordy would refuse to have anything. Then the food would come and Esther would work on Mrs. Gordy until she succumbed. At last they'd head home, where Sam, fresh from his golf or tennis game, would be waiting for them. He would serve them the lunch he had prepared and they would be too polite to tell him they had already eaten. So every day they ate lunch twice and Esther began to gain weight.

Then they would watch a little television until it was time for Mrs. Gordy to leave and Esther would get into bed, and remain there until Mrs. Gordy returned the next day.

27. In early June, Sam took Esther to Dr. Sudhalter for her three-month checkup. He reported that after hearing about her fatigue, the doctor had decided not to reduce the dosage of medication for another three months, but he did change it to another antidepressant, imipramine, which he felt might make her less drowsy.

Over the phone Sam told me that Esther's reaction to the situation distressed him. "She's becoming more listless each day."

I then spoke to Esther. "Hi, darling. I'm fine," she said, doing her best to pretend everything was all right with her.

I pressed her to tell me what was really going on.

"I'm sad," she finally admitted, "that things are taking so long. I don't know whether they'll ever get better. The sadder I get, the more exhausted I feel, and the more exhausted I am, the worse I know I'm getting. I try not to be sad, but the whole situation isn't very good and I can't control my feelings about it."

Sam had done his best to take Esther's mind off her exhaustion. He had suggested a trip, but she said she didn't want to sleep in a hotel room. She didn't want to do anything.

"She's so close to making it," Sam said, "and yet all she does is lie there. Do you remember when she had new ideas all day long and so much energy she couldn't be stopped? We've got to find a way to bring her back."

I promised I would think of something.

I knew I couldn't take her to another psychiatrist. What could he do that had not already been done? Perhaps what was needed was a more radical approach.

I had friends who had tried various new therapies. One, a respected literary agent, suggested that I call Dr. Cynthia King, a leader of the humanistic psychology movement, a respected psychological researcher, and an acknowledged expert in these therapies. I was assured that she would know exactly whom and what to recommend.

From Los Angeles I called Dr. King in New York and described Esther's condition. Making no attempt to diagnose over the phone, she gave me the names of the two people she thought could help.

"My philosophy simply is that all mental conditions usually have a physical as well as a psychological root," she told me. "In order to achieve balance, your mother's body and her mind have to be treated simultaneously. The doctor I recommend to diagnose and correct any imbalances in her system is Dr. Ronald Lawton. I suggest you call him immediately." She rattled off Lawton's telephone number. "The other person to contact is Marie Norton, a young therapist whom I have personally trained. Her specialty is aging and her official title is 'humanistic gerontologist.' She is trained to supply the nurturing your mother might need while she makes the transition back to health."

The two doctors were both in New York and I thought at first that I would have Sam call. But curiosity induced me to call them myself.

I called Marie Norton first. Instantly sympathetic, she quizzed me gently but probingly about Esther's condition. I sensed her involvement and enthusiasm.

"I can't wait to meet your parents," she exclaimed.

"I'll have my father call you."

Then I tried Dr. Lawton's number. His secretary explained that the treatment required a number of visits. She recommended a facility closer to my parents' home, the Long Island Nutritional Therapy Center, where there were doctors who were doing the same kind of work as Lawton.

I called the center and supplied a case history to a

counselor. I then asked her about the center's approach.

"We practice orthomolecular psychiatry," I was told.

"What's that?" I asked.

"You may know it as megavitamin therapy."

I was taken aback. I could just imagine what Esther and Sam were going to think when I told them that humanistic gerontology and megavitamin therapy were next on their agenda.

It was just as I'd anticipated. "Megavitamin therapy? That's crazy!" Sam exploded after he heard my explanation. His doubt exceeded even my expectations.

"We have to try everything," I said. "I'm as skeptical as you are, but we've seen what traditional doctors can do. Now we've got to give some untraditional ones a chance."

Sam promised to call and make the appointments and phone me after each visit.

Esther had always liked being with young people and young people had always reciprocated her enthusiasm. Marie Norton was not only young but also friendly and outgoing. Esther liked her immediately. She responded to her warmth and her smile; she also loved her bright, plant-filled apartment.

Marie watched Sam help Esther off with her coat. Esther did not have much mobility in her arms. She held herself rigid and gasped with effort from the slightest movement. They sat down in Marie's sunny office and talked awhile. Marie began to question Esther, but before Esther was able to frame her response, Sam would answer for her.

Marie told Sam, "I know you are trying to help Esther, but I need her to give her own answers."

Marie said that she and Esther would be working together for about forty-five minutes each week. Then she wanted to spend five or ten minutes working with Sam alone. At the end of the visit, the three of them would talk together. She asked Esther to come into the workroom. Her first objective, she told Esther, was to help her relax. When that was accomplished, it would be time to begin working to encourage Esther to experience once again feelings of happiness and ease.

Marie sat down on a large gym mat and asked Esther to sit beside her. Esther gingerly lowered herself to the floor. The effort made her giggle.

Then Marie began to teach her a series of breathing exercises. They practiced them together for a few minutes until Esther started to loosen up. When they finished the exercises, Esther was breathing more deeply than before. She was also feeling more relaxed.

Marie then began to lead her through a process known as "life review therapy," designed specifically for older patients by the director of the National Institute on Aging, Dr. Robert N. Butler.

Butler believed that the reminiscences of older patients should be encouraged and listened to, because frequently they contained important clues to the unresolved conflicts and basic fears that existed in the life of the patient. By easing these conflicts and fears, a therapist could help make the patient's later life more peaceable. Marie wanted to use this technique to make Esther feel more optimistic about herself.

The first step in the process was to have the patient supply an autobiography. Marie questioned Esther, urging her to remember her past, to describe her earliest memories, to go over her childhood, recalling her feelings for her mother, her father, her brother, her sister.

Delighted by Marie's attention, Esther set about telling the story of her life. Her stories were mainly of a happy, carefree childhood. She did indicate, however, that while her brother and sister had enjoyed specialized educations, she had not displayed much aptitude and therefore had received a more limited education. Though she was sorry she had not had a career, she wasn't unhappy about the way things had worked out. She loved her husband and son; all in all, she had had a good life.

Marie began pointing out all the positive things that had occurred in Esther's life, urging her to make a list of them—year by year, moment by moment, person by person. Esther went to work on the assignment. "The list is endless!" she exclaimed. Marie then urged her to recall the good feelings that accompanied each of these moments, and let them fill her mind and her body.

Concentrating Esther began to laugh. "I suddenly have so many good feelings in me," she announced, "I think I'm going to explode."

Esther's work was over for the first session. Sam and Marie then talked privately. Marie listened attentively as Sam, responding to her obvious interest, described his own problems.

Marie told Sam that he had been through so much he now was attempting to protect himself against any further trouble by covering up for Esther in public, seeking to control an uncontrollable situation.

"As painful as it is," said Marie, "you have to let her stammer on her own if she is going to learn to speak again. She has to feel well enough about herself to think she can help herself. And then she will."

Then Marie called Esther into the room and helped her on with her coat. A second appointment was made. At the door, Marie hugged and kissed Esther.

"What about my husband?" Esther said suddenly. "Hug him too."

Marie gave Sam a big hug. Grinning boyishly, he hugged her back.

The walls of the Long Island Nutritional Therapy Center were decorated with large, striking photorealist paintings of luscious-looking strawberries, oranges and grapes. Esther and Sam sat under the grapes, listening to Eleanor Chass, the center's director. "We believe first and foremost that the patient's nutritional chemistry must be brought to peak condition before any kind of therapy can work successfully," she told them. "We also believe that mental illness often disappears after the body is properly nourished for a sufficient amount of time. Therefore, we set out first to correct such biochemical abnormalities in the body as vitamin, mineral, trace mineral and amino acid imbalances. We also immediately diagnose and treat illnesses that create nutritional imbalances, illnesses like hypoglycemia, a condition in which the level of sugar in the blood is abnormally low, causing depression and other mental problems. And that's what we want to do for you: carry out a thorough nutritional work-up, then help you bring your nutrition to peak condition."

Mrs. Chass introduced Esther to Mrs. Bergen, a social worker who would take her case history.

Once again Esther was questioned about her family, her medical history, her marriage. She was asked about her hospitalizations and the medications she was taking. She described her sleep patterns and said she felt exhausted when she got up in the morning. She also described her eating patterns and told Mrs. Bergen she had an insatiable craving for sweets.

"Why don't you tell us why you are here?"

Esther listed her symptoms: a poor memory, poor concentration, the inability to get up until ten or eleven in the morning, a feeling of numbness in her hands, a continual sensation of cold even though it was summer, a lack of pleasure from the things she used to like, such as looking at pictures and collecting antiques, breaking into a cold sweat after meals.

Mrs. Bergen recommended a complete diagnostic work-up, consisting of blood tests, a hair analysis, in which a lock of hair would be examined chemically to determine which minerals and trace minerals were missing from Esther's body, a urinalysis, a complete physical examination and an electroencephalogram.

The center decided that Esther's symptoms—her chronic fatigue, her craving for sweets, and the short highs and subsequent devastating lows that occurred whenever she ate sugar—were proof that she had hypoglycemia and she was not given the exhausting glucose tolerance test, a five-hour procedure during which she would have had to ingest one hundred grams of sugar and undergo five blood tests—one per hour—to determine how effectively her body digested the sugar.

A lock of hair and a blood and a urine specimen were sent to the labs. Once again, as in her earliest days at Chelsea, electrodes were attached to her skull and she was given an electroencephalogram.

Two weeks later the results arrived. Esther and Sam met with Frederick Johnson, one of the center's psychiatrists. The EEG was normal, as were the blood and urine tests. The hair analysis, however, indicated that her body possessed excessive amounts of magnesium, sodium, potassium and selenium, and insufficient manganese, zinc and chromium.

Years before, Esther had undergone four years of cortisone and steroid therapy for asthma. Dr. Johnson believed this had left her body chemistry seriously out of balance.

To rectify the condition, he prescribed a vitamin/ mineral program supplemented by the psychiatric medication she was currently taking, as well as supportive counseling, which she would receive from him at the center. He also explained that psychiatric medication stimulated the appetite center of the brain, so that Esther had to become extremely weight conscious. He put her on a strict hypoglycemia diet, which would control her digestion of concentrated sugars and also help her lose weight. The diet consisted almost exclusively of proteins, with small portions of low-carbohydrate foods and a complete absence of all processed carbohydrates, such as sugar and white flour. Caffeine was also restricted and, naturally, all candies, baked goods and ice cream were strictly forbidden. Esther found this the hardest part.

The center dispensed its own megavitamins, and two of their formulas, as well as dolomite, a natural substance composed of calcium and magnesium, were prescribed for Esther. Johnson told Esther that by taking these vitamins and minerals, she would start supplying her body with the chemicals it needed to function properly. She was to return in a month to report her progress.

Sam picked up the vitamins at the dispensary. When she got home, Esther took out the bottles, opened them, and poured the capsules on the dining room table. She and Mrs. Gordy stared at them in disbelief. The capsules were huge. "They look like rocks," Esther said in disgust.

Mrs. Gordy shrugged her shoulders.

"They're supposed to make me sane."

In the morning and in the evening, Esther wrestled down the "rocks."

"Sam," she'd call out, "I can feel them in my stomach.

Each time I take a step, they shift from left to right."

Would the "rocks" help? Who knew? No matter what they had been through, Esther and Sam had never expected their search for help to lead them to giant-sized capsules and huge tablets of dolomite.

One of Esther's favorite activities with Marie was something Marie called a "mind game." It was one of a series of exercises designed by Jean Houston and her husband, Robert Masters, the directors of the Foundation for Mind Research. The exercise was designed to stimulate the imagination and increase mental capacity. The fantasy and the poetry of the exercise appealed to Esther. First Marie helped her to relax thoroughly. Then she was asked to imagine a childlike fantasy, a dream in which she got into a boat and floated downstream on a warm, sunlit, breeze-filled day.

The exercise was filled with wonderful, sparkling images.

" 'Be aware of this whole situation—the movements, the warmth, the sounds, the odors—as you keep on drifting down and down.' "

Marie paused to allow Esther to experience the images. There was total stillness in the room. When she felt that Esther was ready to move on, she started again.

" 'Continue now to float,' " Marie said softly, " 'to rock, gently, drifting deeper and deeper, until your boat approaches the shore and runs smoothly aground at the edge of a meadow. Leaving the boat now, and walking through the meadow, the grass against your legs, the breezes on your body, and conscious of rabbits in the tall grass, of the smell of the flowers all around, of birds singing in the trees, of the movements of your body as you walk, approaching a large tree and seating yourself beneath it, in its shade.

" 'Sit there now, taking pleasure in all this, enjoying it just as completely as you can. . . .' "

Esther was smiling.

"Wake up!"

"It was lovely," Esther announced, "just lovely."

"What was lovely?" Marie asked.

"The meadow. I loved the meadow."

Esther had made an excursion on her own. Marie was curious. "Tell me about it."

"It was filled with daisies," Esther said.

"Daisies?"

"I love daisies. If it were up to me, I'd put daisies everywhere."

"Why?"

"They're cheerful. If there were daisies everywhere, everyone would have to be more cheerful."

"You like to cheer people up."

"Yes."

"What else would you like to do?"

Esther thought for a moment. "I'd like to work in a foundling hospital."

"What would you do there?"

"I'd hold the babies. They need to be held. They need to be loved. Simply by holding them and stroking them and kissing them, I know I could do them some good."

"In your life have you given enough love?"

"You can never give enough love."

"Have you been loved enough?"

"My husband loves me; my son loves me; but what does enough mean? When I was sick I couldn't accept the love they were giving and I couldn't give them the love they needed. So I don't know what enough means; but I do know I love my family a lot."

28. Before he was ready to leave one morning, Sam told Esther, "There's a very strong wind out there. I think you should stay in today."

Esther looked disappointed. She was proud of herself because she had developed the regimen of getting out of the house. It was a good way of beating the fatigue. She was afraid that if she missed her walk even for one day, she would undo the progress she had made and her discipline would begin to crumble.

After Sam left, Esther turned to Mrs. Gordy. "I want to go out," she said. "Let's take a shorter walk today. We'll just go to the park and back."

The women bundled themselves up. As soon as they stepped outside, they were enveloped by the wind. Esther did her best to make small talk, reassuring Mrs. Gordy that they would make it.

Finally, they reached the edge of Woodrow Wilson Park. The wind became suddenly stronger.

Esther looked at Mrs. Gordy. Mrs. Gordy looked at Esther. They tightened their grip on each other, but it was no use. The wind had become too strong. No matter how hard they tried, they could only march in place.

"O Lord," beseeched Mrs. Gordy, "please don't make it a hurricane!"

"We'll make it!" Esther said, with as much jauntiness as she could muster. She was convinced she was a goner.

Just then, a gigantic gust of wind came speeding down on Esther, reaching out and pushing at her chest. Like a toy soldier in slow motion, she fell backward onto the grass, taking Mrs. Gordy with her.

The women weren't hurt. They realized that. But they were frightened, and what frightened them most was the fact that neither was strong enough to get up.

They began to rock back and forth, hoping that the momentum would help them to get back on their feet, but their rocking got them nowhere. They looked around. The park was deserted and there was no one to rescue them, no one to hear their cries for help.

Mrs. Gordy began to pray. "Please, Lord, spare us. I was the nurse. I should have been responsible. I'm prepared to take all the blame." Then she added, "But I'm not a bad lady and I've always meant well and I'm sure you'll agree that this is no way for either of us to go." They sat there, embarrassed, powerless, afraid, trying their best to comfort each other, and feeling terrible.

Esther had a sudden change of heart. "Enough! Enough!" she said. "If no one can help us, then we have to help ourselves."

She began to crawl on her hands and knees. Across the grass she crawled, while the wind blew all around her. The wind brought tears to her eyes, but she kept on. She imagined what she must look like, crawling on the ground, and the image made her giggle in spite of herself. Finally, she got to a park bench. Using first the seat of the bench as a support and then its arms, slowly she hoisted herself to her feet. She felt triumphant.

"Now I'm ready for the Olympics." She walked back to Mrs. Gordy and extended her arms. Pulling with all her might, she slowly helped her up.

The wind still blew around them, but now they were impervious to it. They had met disaster and had stared it down. Arm in arm, they marched to the ice cream parlor and ordered hot fudge sundaes. "Make them doubles," Esther said.

When they got home, they described their adventure to Sam. He was shocked by what had happened but he was even more appalled by the fact that they found it so amusing.

"You're very lucky," he said. "You could have been hurt."

They laughed even harder.

"I told you not to go out. Don't you see what happens when you don't listen?"

"I loved every second of it," Esther gasped.

"No one takes anything seriously around here. That's why you're always getting into trouble."

"That's true! That's true!" Esther looked at Mrs. Gordy. They started to laugh again. "Don't worry. You know us! We won't rest until we find some new trouble to get into."

29. After dutifully swallowing megavitamins for a month, Esther returned to the Long Island Nutritional Therapy Center.

Dr. Johnson asked if she had been careful about following the diet and if she had noticed any changes in the way she felt.

"I cheated on the hypoglycemia diet," she admitted. "I had ice cream."

"Only once?"

"No. A number of times."

"Is there anything else?"

"The vitamins have increased my appetite. I've never been hungrier in my entire life."

Dr. Johnson explained once again that he believed the psychiatric medication she was taking was the primary cause of her hunger. "When you are taking medication and vitamins," he reminded her, "it's even more important for you to stay on your diet."

"I went to the movies for the first time last weekend and I sat through the entire show," she continued.

"How was the movie?"

"I enjoyed it."

Dr. Johnson turned to Sam. "What about her fatigue and lack of concentration?"

"She still can't function in the morning," Sam reported. "She still gets tired quickly. But she does take longer walks and goes out more often with me and she looks better and does more talking."

"That's real improvement," said the doctor. He advised them to continue with the two formulas she had been taking, increasing one of them to two pills a day, and he added "Formula I," a fifty-milligram tablet of zinc.

After they had picked up the zinc tablets and left the center, Esther turned to Sam. "I try to be very good about taking those pills, but I can't bear to swallow any more of them. The sides of my throat hurt."

Sam agreed to allow Esther a month off. If she continued to improve without the vitamins, she would not have to take them anymore; if not, she would resume taking them.

"I'm going to do fine without them," Esther said.

"We've had ten sessions together," Marie told Esther and Sam, "and I think the time has come for you to see two other therapists who can give you the special help you need."

Esther did not want to leave Marie, but Marie assured her that they would keep in close touch with each other and always remain friends. She added that she would also keep in contact with Esther's new therapists.

"One is Dr. Joanna Walden, your nutritional psychotherapist," Marie continued. "She will help you with your constant feelings of hunger and help you learn to control your appetite. As you learn to control your hunger, Esther, you will be learning once again to control your life.

"The other is Art Nulty. He teaches the Feldenkrais method."

"The what?"

"The Feldenkrais method is a system of exercises invented by an Israeli therapist named Moshe Feldenkrais. These exercises will make you more aware of your body and the way you move. As you do them, your own awareness will grow and you will become more confident. Your breathing will also improve."

Marie put her arm around Esther. "You should be really proud," she told her. "We've gone forward together and now you're ready to go out and meet people who will take you even further."

"Thank you for everything you've done," Esther said softly. "I'm going to miss you very much."

At the elevator, Esther turned. "I love you," she said to Marie. Then she waved goodbye.

The following Tuesday, Esther had her first meeting with her nutritional psychotherapist. They hit it off immediately. Dr. Joanna Walden and she talked about antiques, soap operas, and vacation trips to Maine. Joanna, as she asked Esther to call her, gave Esther a lengthy form on which was listed every conceivable kind of food. Esther was to put a check next to the foods she liked best. Then, insofar as possible, Joanna tried to include Esther's favorite foods in the diet she constructed for her.

Esther promised to follow this new diet strictly. An appointment was made for her to return in a week's time.

Two days later, she had her first meeting with her Feldenkrais teacher.

Art Nulty threw open the door and stepped past Sam, who stood protectively in front of his wife.

"Hello, Esther," he announced as he shook her hand. "I'm Art Nulty. It's nice to see you." He escorted Esther into his apartment. It reminded her of Marie's apartment, filled as it was with sunlight and plants. Esther felt at home.

Art observed Esther's restricted breathing and the rigidity of her whole body. He could see that she had difficulty turning her head to the left or right. As a Feldenkrais teacher, Art believed that there was an intimate connection between mind and body which people were just beginning to discover. The body could be made to talk to the mind and send it messages of change. As an individual got rid of restrictions of the body, the mind would become freer.

Art knew that when people were physically weak, it made them psychologically weak. He believed that as Esther's body grew stronger, she would realize that she had the inner strength to deal with the things that troubled her.

"You're going to learn how to relax. You're also going to become more flexible and improve your balance," he told her. "Sam, you can do them too," he said, as he began to put Esther through a series of twisting movements. Sam, ever the exercise buff, joined in enthusiastically. The teacher concentrated on making Esther aware of each part of her body. Slowly, limb by limb, he made her feel each of her movements, and the more aware of her movements she became, the more movement she was able to perform.

Art was determined to make Esther capable of moving her head and shoulders separately. At the end of the session, she could.

"I guess I'm getting better," Esther said on the ride home. "I can move my head."

The next Tuesday, at Joanna's, Esther confessed that she loved her new diet, which even had ice cream on it. She claimed that she had followed it with the utmost precision, but when Joanna weighed her, she had gained a pound.

Joanna and she had another long chat and Joanna urged her to try even harder during the following week.

Esther assured her that she would.

On Thursday she returned to Art's. At this session they began to work on some breathing exercises. First they reviewed what Marie had taught Esther. Then they did some exercises to help Esther breathe more deeply and regularly.

"Now, doing these once a week isn't enough," Art told her. "You've got to do some work on your own. I've got a tape for you, a tape recorded by Moshe Feldenkrais himself. These are a series of exercises you can do every day at home."

Esther was excited. She couldn't wait to get home and hit the living room rug with Mrs. Gordy and Sam.

As soon as she burst through the door, she declared, "I've got my very own Feldenkrais tape. Let's go to work."

Sam put the tape on and Dr. Feldenkrais's heavily accented voice flooded the room:

"Here you will learn to increase the contraction of the erector muscles of the back, and that prolonged contraction of the flexor muscles of the abdomen increases the tonus of the extensors of the back."

Esther began to laugh.

"You will be able to lengthen the muscles that twist the body. Lengthening the extensors of the nape by activating their antagonists in the front of the neck improves the balance of the head in the erect standing position. You will also learn improved differentiation of head and trunk movement.

"Lie on your back, stretch out your legs, feet apart. Bend your knees and cross your legs, placing the right over the left. . . ."

Following directions, Esther, Mrs. Gordy and Sam lowered themselves onto the floor.

"Let both knees drop down to the floor toward the right, so that both are now supported by the left foot only. The weight of the right leg will help both legs sink to the right toward the floor. . . . "

They did the best they could.

"Now let your knees return to the neutral or middle position, then let them drop to the right again."

Esther was confused. So was Mrs. Gordy. Sam, however, forged on.

"Repeat twenty-five times."

Esther sat on the floor and counted out loud as Sam did the exercise. Occasionally, Mrs. Gordy counted too.

For forty-five minutes Sam urged them to join him as he did the exercises.

Day after day the pattern was the same. "Exercise time," Esther would announce, and she would start doing the exercises. But after the first ten minutes, Sam was the only one still exercising, while Esther and Mrs. Gordy watched.

Once a week, Esther would be weighed by Joanna. They talked about Esther's difficulty in controlling her food intake. Each week Esther swore that she had been faithful to the diet. Each week she gained a pound.

In five weeks, she had gained five pounds.

"I don't think I can help you," Joanna said sadly. "I just don't think I can do a thing."

"Don't worry about it," Esther replied. "It's a lovely diet. I'm sure it will do somebody some good someday."

"That the first and last time I'll ever pay anybody one hundred and fifty-five dollars so you can gain five pounds," Sam said as they walked toward the car.

"Don't be such a spoilsport," Esther replied. "It was an experience. Experiences always cost money."

Also at the end of five weeks, Art asked Esther for a report.

Sam spoke first. "My body is straighter," he said. "My shoulders feel less tense. I'm breathing more deeply than I've ever breathed before."

"And you, Esther?"

"They're wonderful exercises. The best. No wonder I'm beginning to shape up. They're the best exercises I've ever done."

Sam stared at Esther. He was about to open his mouth, when Esther threw him a look that defied him to say a word.

"You're improving without doing much of the work," Sam said on the way home. "Think of how much you'd improve if you really did them."

"The exercises I don't do on the floor I do in my mind," Esther replied, "and that's more exercise than I ever had before. Think of all the years I didn't do any exercise up there at all."

30. Mrs. Gordy's eyes were swollen from crying. Sam made some gentle inquiries as he let her into the apartment, but he could see that she didn't want to talk.

"Something is wrong," he whispered to Esther.

"I'll take care of it," Esther whispered in reply. "Go play golf."

"Are you sure?"

"I'm sure."

"The minute I'm out of the house, I know you'll be calling me to come home."

"That's not true. Go!"

Sam headed for the golf course, and Esther made Mrs. Gordy a cup of tea. They began to talk. Esther couldn't believe what she was hearing.

Mrs. Gordy described a terrible fight she had had with Willy. Willy had accused her of trying to turn Sally against him. In a fit of rage, he had forbidden Sally or the children to have any more to do with her. Sally, caught in the middle, had done her best to calm him down. But it was impossible. "I want that old hag out in two weeks," Willy had bellowed. Then he'd dashed into Mrs. Gordy's room and screamed in her face. "Get out of here, old lady!"

Mrs. Gordy had known she would have to move eventually, but now she knew she would have to move at once.

She began to weep openly. "I'm an old woman," she sobbed, "and I have no place to go."

"As soon as Sam comes home," said Esther, "we'll go apartment hunting. I've moved six times in my lifetime. It's always fun. It gives you the opportunity to decorate a new apartment. I'll help you. Think of the lovely job we'll do."

"I can't afford to move," said Mrs. Gordy.

"We'll find you a place you can afford."

When Sam got home, Esther announced determinedly, "We're going apartment hunting. Mrs. Gordy has got to get out of her house immediately."

"Where will we look?" asked Sam.

"Where would you like to live?" Esther asked Mrs. Gordy.

"I'd like to live near my church."

Esther said, "We'll use the church as a target zone."

They set out immediately to Mrs. Gordy's church. Then Sam began to cruise the streets of the neighborhood, looking for For Rent signs. They searched for three hours and found only two apartments and they were both too expensive.

The next day they set out again. This time they went to realtors. When Mrs. Gordy told the realtors how much rent she could afford, the first one said he couldn't help her at all; the second, more sympathetic, said it would take a long time. The result was the same: no apartment.

After they had looked fruitlessly for a few more days, Esther told Mrs. Gordy there had to be a social agency that would help. "Let's let our fingers do the walking," she said, grabbing the yellow pages. Esther found the address of the community agency that served the neighborhood surrounding the church, and soon after, they arrived on its doorstep.

All eyes turned to stare at the three senior citizens as they stepped into the building. Esther, Sam and Mrs. Gordy headed for the receptionist.

"What can I do for you?" she asked.

"We need some information," Sam replied.

She handed them a number. "We'll call you," she said.

They retired to a bench and settled in for almost an hour. During that time, Sam read his newspaper. Esther and Mrs. Gordy, meanwhile, had a number of pleasant conversations—with a deserted mother, an unwed pregnant teen-ager, and an elderly man with cataracts who could not afford new glasses.

Finally their number was called. They introduced themselves to Mr. Henderson, a weary, gray-haired social worker. He listened as they told the story of Mrs. Gordy's imminent eviction.

The social worker asked Mrs. Gordy a number of questions about her finances. "You're lucky," he told her. "Another few dollars and you wouldn't qualify for a senior citizens' apartment house only a few minutes from here."

Mr. Henderson called the building and learned that there was a vacancy coming up on the first of the month. "There's a long waiting list," he said, "but I suggest you go over there now and see the superintendent. Ask for Mr. Donald." He handed Sam the address.

"Sam, let's go," ordered Esther, "before we lose it to someone else."

They zoomed off. Eight minutes later, they were ringing Mr. Donald's bell. The superintendent came to the door.

"This is Mrs. Gordy," said Esther. "Mr. Henderson just told you about her. May we see the apartment?"

"The lady who lives there is out for the day, so it will be my pleasure to show it to you," the superintendent replied. "She's going to California to live with her daughter." He got his keys and led the group to the third-floor apartment. He opened the door and they stepped in. The apartment was small but bright.

Mrs. Gordy smiled appreciatively. She could see that it would make a lovely home.

Meanwhile Esther and Sam gave the apartment a thorough going over. They checked the closets, the refrigerator and the stove. They made sure the windows did not stick.

Sam sidled up to Mr. Donald. They stepped into a corner and began to whisper.

Mr. Donald shook his head in disbelief. "Why would anyone do that to a small old lady like that? It's shocking!"

Esther echoed Mr. Donald's reaction from the other side of the room. "It's more than a shame," she exclaimed. "It's the shame of shames!"

"What's the rent?" asked Sam.

It was within Mrs. Gordy's means.

They all trooped down to Mr. Donald's office. Mrs. Gordy filled out the application slowly, writing in delicate, extremely legible script. When she had a question, she would turn to Esther and Sam. Finally, they had it complete.

Mr. Donald looked over the application. He smiled at the trio. "I think that very soon Mrs. Gordy will be a new tenant of ours."

"Wonderful," said Sam.

The women were hungry. Sam drove them to the ice cream parlor, where they all feasted on chicken salad sandwiches and celebrated with hot fudge sundaes.

That evening, Mrs. Gordy went to her church. She described the events of the day to Dr. Smith and the members of the congregation.

"Let us pray for Mrs. Katz," said the minister.

"I pray that Mrs. Katz fully recovers," Mrs. Gordy said out loud. "I pray that she gets complete control of her body, that all of her energy comes back, that she finishes off the rest of her life in a happy, lively, healthy fashion."

Dr. Smith touched Mrs. Gordy on the shoulder. "Why
don't you invite your friends to one of our Sunday services and dinners?"

The next day Mrs. Gordy extended an invitation.

"I'm not up to it yet," Esther replied. "I'd like to go,
but I'm not ready. I need more time."

"I'll wait," said Mrs. Gordy. Then she added, "And I
know you're going to make it. That's going to be a day
none of us will ever forget!"

31. There was no doubt about it: Esther had improved. She stayed up longer. She would occasionally go with Sam on those days when
he could persuade Mrs. Gordy to allow him to drive
her to her new apartment in the early afternoon when
her morning's work was over. Less often, she would
drive with Sam into Manhattan and visit a favorite de-
partment store. But Esther's fatigue persisted and she
still remained in bed almost half the day. Every time
she encountered a person who was concerned and could
project that concern, she responded. What had also
helped was her friendship with Mrs. Gordy, about
whom she could be concerned and for whom she could
be strong. Sam, of course, had been a tower of strength.

Still, going out to visit friends was a trial to her,
though she liked having them to the house. And in the
early evenings, when she was too worn down to go anywhere, she would grow depressed. It was six months
since the second hospitalization and Dr. Sudhalter had
not reduced the medication yet, proof, she believed, that
this was as far as she could go.

One evening I called. Esther seemed pensive.

"What are you thinking about?" I asked.

"I'm thinking about how hard I'm trying and yet how hard it is for me to get all better."

"Do *you* think you'll get all better?"

"Do you want to hear the truth?"

"Sure."

"I think this may be as far as I can go."

"What makes you say that?"

"Because I'm trying with all my might and I'm still getting nowhere. I never wanted to be a burden. I never wanted to make anybody unhappy. But I've been a burden for almost a year. When I get too tired to go on, I'm even a burden to myself. What's happening to me makes me sad, but I don't want to burden you with it anymore. What you and Sam have gone through with me also makes me sad. But if my problems are always on your mind, I'll feel the saddest of all. What is important is that you do well in Los Angeles and do what you have to do without worrying about me. The only thing that will make me feel good these days is the news that you're well and happy. That's the only news I want to hear."

The filming of *Sgt. Pepper's Lonely Hearts Club Band* began on a sunny day at the end of August. On the MGM studio backlot in Culver City, California, the original small-town setting used in the MGM Andy Hardy film series of the 1940s had been transformed for the occasion into a freshly painted pastel-tinted vision of contemporary small-town Americana. Gathered together on the set were George Burns, Steve Martin, the Bee Gees, Peter Frampton, Aerosmith, and Earth, Wind and Fire, all eager to begin the first day's work.

I called Esther and Sam nearly every day, and began

to notice that Sam sounded tired. I urged him to get out of the house more. After all, that's why Mrs. Gordy had been hired. But he still couldn't stay away for more than a couple of hours at a time without feeling guilty.

With each day he sounded wearier. I couldn't understand it. According to Sam, Esther's health remained the same. On the other hand, she hadn't gotten worse. I thought that perhaps here was a chance for him to really feel his own fatigue in the breathing space that her stabilized condition provided. I told him he sounded tired.

"I'm sorry," he said. "It must be catching."

Sam, who had never complained, began to complain of an itch, an itch on various areas of his body, an itch so severe it was driving him mad. His description reminded me of a condition I had once had. It had been caused by dry skin and, on a dermatologist's advice, had been successfully treated with bath oils, oil-based soaps and gooey creams. I told Sam to stock up.

"I took your advice," he reported a few days later, "but none of this stuff is doing any good. It's getting worse. I'm still in agony."

Esther got on the phone. "It's awful," she said. "He can't sleep. He's scratched himself raw. When he gets up in the morning, there are bloodstains on the sheets."

"I'd like you to go to a doctor," I suggested. "You go to a lot of gyms and shower a lot in public places. Maybe you picked something up. Did you call your internist?"

"Dr. Northrup is on vacation."

"Go to someone in the neighborhood."

Sam made an appointment with Dr. Gerald Schwimmer, an internist in a nearby medical center.

Schwimmer examined Sam and could not determine the cause of the itch. He suggested that Sam see a dermatologist in the same medical center.

Sam went around the corner to Andrew Bernstein's office. Dr. Bernstein was also at a loss to explain the itch. However, he did prescribe triamcinolone ointment, a cortisone-like drug that relieves inflammation.

The ointment did not work. Dr. Bernstein prescribed another ointment, then changed the prescription once again when the second did not work. When Sam came back again, he said, "Let's attack it from another side. These things are very tricky." He prescribed a lotion that killed parasites. Before bed, Sam had to cover his entire body with the thick white substance. In the morning he was to wash it off. Esther helped rub it into his back. Sam performed that ritual for two nights; the itch grew worse.

The dermatologist decided to perform a biopsy, just to make sure that Sam did not have skin cancer. "It's a precaution," he told Sam. A small section of skin was frozen; then a specimen a mere one cell thick was removed and sent to the laboratory for analysis.

The results were negative. Sam returned to Dr. Schwimmer, who made an appointment for Sam to go to the laboratory the following morning for a GI series—X rays of Sam's gastrointestinal region—as well as a blood test. At dawn the next day Sam rose and went to the medical testing center. He was given a glass of thick white barium solution to drink. Then the X rays were taken and blood was drawn.

A week later, I got a call from him. "I have to go to the hospital," he told me.

"Why?"

"To get a liver biopsy," he replied. "It's nothing. Dr. Northrup is back from his vacation. He's going to do it."

"Whose idea is this?"

"Originally Dr. Schwimmer's."

"Why do you need a liver biopsy?"

"They aren't satisfied with the results of my liver tests. It's nothing," he added almost defensively. "Just routine."

Esther suddenly got on the line. "I'm worried," she said, and she sounded it.

"Don't worry," I replied. "I'm going to find out exactly what is going on."

I got Schwimmer's telephone number from Sam and called the doctor. "My father tells me he is having a liver biopsy," I said. "Can you tell me why?"

"We've conducted a GI series on him, as well as a series of blood tests. His liver scores are high, indicating that the liver is malfunctioning and that there may be liver damage. The X rays also look suspicious."

"What are your suspicions?"

"Chronic itching sometimes indicates the presence of cancer of the pancreas that has spread to the liver. The cancer eats through the bile duct, causing the bile to flow directly into the bloodstream. That's the reason for the itch. A liver biopsy will tell us whether our suspicions are true."

"Do you think my father has cancer?"

"As I said before, his abnormally high liver scores as well as his X rays are suspicious."

"Suppose the liver biopsy confirms those suspicions?"

"By the time pancreatic cancer is diagnosed, it almost always is terminal."

I hung up the phone. Numb, I sat there for what seemed like hours, unable to move, unable to think coherently. Finally, I pulled myself together enough to plan a course of action. Just as I had had to leave Bermuda immediately a year ago, now I had to fly back to New York at once. I wanted to be with my parents. Esther's hospital experience had taught me the value of a second opinion. I also wanted to be there to get another doctor.

I picked up the phone and called Esther and Sam. "Hi," I said. "I've finally reached Dr. Schwimmer. You're right; it is a routine procedure they're doing, just to make sure that absolutely nothing is wrong."

"Are you sure?" Esther asked.

"Sure I'm sure. But I know you. You're going to worry no matter what anybody tells you. I'm going to fly in and keep you company while Sam has his day in the hospital. How's that?"

Esther was delighted. I told them I would take the "Red Eye," the night flight that left Los Angeles at ten-thirty in the evening and arrived in New York at six the following morning. Sam said he would meet me at the airport.

Most passengers on the Red Eye manage to fall asleep the minute the plane takes off and remain asleep until arrival. As a commuter, I, too, had trained myself to go to sleep on the Red Eye without difficulty. This time, however, my mind raced frantically throughout the entire flight. I could not believe that Sam might now be very sick. It was too unjust. I could not even begin to think about the effect this would have on Esther if it were true. I could not begin to think of the effect it would have on me.

Sam was waiting in the terminal as I stepped off the plane. We hugged each other. I could see that his face, neck and arms were covered with deep red welts. He had lost weight and looked exhausted. Involuntarily, he would start to scratch a welt and then he would stop himself. "They're driving me mad," he said.

We stood at the baggage claim waiting for my luggage to come down the chute. As one of my suitcases passed on the conveyor belt, I reached out and grabbed it. Sam took it from me.

"Please put it down," I said, but I could not stop him. He was happy only when he was being helpful. And now he was determined to help me.

By now it was about eight in the morning and we quickly made the drive to the apartment.

"My illness makes no sense," he told me on the way. "I've been suffering for two months and no one can figure out a thing. Yesterday Dr. Northrup even took me off my blood pressure medication in case I've become allergic to it. Tomorrow is just another wild-goose chase. But what am I supposed to do?"

"I'm going to call Dr. Northrup and see if I can get some more information," I replied.

"That's a good idea, he said. "He hasn't told me much at all."

I assumed that Stanley Northrup, not wanting to tell Sam his suspicions, had been deliberately vague.

Esther threw open the door as soon as she heard us approach. I gave her a hug and a kiss, hugged Mrs. Gordy, and we all sat down to coffee and cake.

"Before you say anything," Esther told me with a laugh, "I'm going to tell you something. I'm going to be fine while Sam is away. So don't ask how I'm going to do."

It had been arranged that Mrs. Gordy would stay the two nights Sam was in the hospital, and the women kept assuring us that they would take good care of themselves. They would go walking and shopping and out to dinner and to the movies.

I watched Esther bringing more coffee. She was determined to show us that she could hold her own. "I'll be fine," she said over and over again.

The fact that Sam was sick had motivated her to relieve him of some of his burdens and she was touching as she set out to convince him that if he had anything to worry about it wasn't her.

I told Sam that I wanted to take my luggage home, but would be back later in the day to have dinner and spend the night and then drive him to the hospital the next morning. Sam insisted that I take the car.

When I got home I didn't want to call Northrup because I was afraid of what I might hear. So as soon as I got into my apartment, instead of making the call, I made myself a cup of coffee and turned on the radio. Then I sat down at the window and spent a long time staring at the parking lot across the street.

Finally, I dialed Northrup's number.

His secretary answered the phone. "This is Mr. Katz's son, Henry," I said. "I'd like to speak to the doctor about my father's operation tomorrow."

"He's not available now," she replied. "I'll tell him you called." She was about to hang up.

"When can I speak to him?"

"The doctor is very busy."

"I understand," I replied. "It will only take a few minutes."

"I'll give him your message."

I waited an hour and called back. "This is Mr. Katz's son again—"

The secretary cut me off. "I haven't had a chance to give the doctor your message."

"When will you have time?"

"Sometime this afternoon." She hung up.

In the middle of the afternoon I called again. This time I was put through.

"Hello, Dr. Northrup, I've just gotten into town to be

with my father during this biopsy," I began. "Dr. Schwimmer indicated that the purpose of this operation is to verify a diagnosis of cancer. I'd like to hear your opinion."

"I'm not going to discuss your father's case with you," Northrup replied. "You're not my patient."

"My father tells me that you told him this is a routine procedure. *Is* it routine?"

"I've given your father the reasons for this procedure. That's all I have to say."

"You wouldn't lie to him, would you?" I asked.

"What leads you to believe I wouldn't tell him the truth?"

"The answer is very simple, Dr. Northrup. My mother went into the most reputable mental institution in New York City and came out with a broken ankle and Parkinsonism. Now another doctor told me that the biopsy is to confirm a diagnosis of cancer. And you won't tell me anything at all. Do you blame me for not trusting you or any other member of your profession?"

"Mr. Edwards, I'm a very busy man. I consider this conversation ended." He hung up.

I called my own internist and described my conversation with Northrup. "There is the chance that there is a cancer," he told me, "but more than likely the biopsy will be normal and they'll have to keep looking for something else.

"If they suspect cancer they'd be better off doing a liver scan which would deliver a picture of the entire liver. The biopsy needle could entirely bypass the cancerous section."

"Should I have them do it? That's all I want to know."

"It wouldn't hurt," he said, "but it might not help."

I had my second opinion.

That night I slept on my parents' sofa, just as I had a year ago on the night before we took Esther to Chelsea Hospital.

In the morning, Mrs. Gordy came early. She and Esther were like two schoolgirls about to have a pajama party while their parents are away.

"We'll take care of everything," Esther kept reassuring Sam as he compulsively went over last-minute details with her, making sure she knew where the checkbook was and had enough cash for the two days he would be away.

"We'll be fine," she told Sam again.

He looked around nervously. Had he forgotten anything? How could things run without him? Was there anything else he had to discuss?

Finally, he knew he had to go. He picked up his satchel of itch creams in case a doctor wanted to see his medications, and we set out for Brookdale Hospital.

At the hospital, Sam checked in and was taken to his room. He changed into his pajamas. His blood pressure was tested and a blood specimen collected.

I kept asking for Dr. Northrup, but he did not appear. Sam urged me to leave, but I stayed put for almost four hours before I gave up.

That night Sam called. Northrup had finally appeared and had assured Sam that all would go well. Sam later told me that he had slept calmly that night; I didn't sleep at all.

The following morning, Northrup arrived at Sam's room at dawn. Sam stood up and faced the doctor. A nurse stood to his left. A painkiller was injected on the right-hand side of Sam's rib cage. A long, thin hollow tube was placed against his ribs. In one quick punching action, a hollow needle within that tube shot through Sam's skin, piercing his liver and removing a microscopic specimen of tissue. The process was almost pain-less, although the force of the punching action—like a swift kick to the stomach—had made him fall against the nurse, who was there to steady him.

At the end of the day, Dr. Northrup reported that the biopsy revealed nothing was wrong with Sam's liver, even though his liver scores remained high.

That evening when I came to see him, Sam gave me the news and I breathed a huge sigh of relief.

The next morning, Sam was still scratching when I picked him up to take him home.

"I knew this was going to be a wild-goose chase," he repeated as we headed for Long Island.

"Were you worried?" I asked.

"No," he replied. "I just felt that these very nice days were being interrupted. A year ago, there was no Esther. Now there's more than half of her. And I'm grate-ful for it. I want to enjoy every minute with her that I can."

A week later, Dr. Northrup called Sam at home. "I think your itch was caused by an allergic reaction to your old blood pressure pill," he told Sam.

As the days went by, the itch began to fade away, the welts to heal. Sam's liver scores eventually returned to normal.

Itching is a basic symptom of allergy. When a patient complains of an itch, the normal practice is to ask him about the medications he is taking. If there is any chance that a patient is having an allergic reaction to the medication, it is changed immediately.

Had Sam's blood pressure pill been taken away the first time he complained, he would have been spared all of the suffering as well as the biopsy. I would have been spared the emergency trip home as well as the alarming report that Sam was terminally ill.

This oversight flabbergasted and then infuriated me. Why had either of my parents been a victim of the medical profession? Why was any patient a victim of the doctors who served him?

32. During the next four months, there was so much work to do on *Sgt. Pepper* that I hardly had time to think. The movie was filmed all day until six, when work would stop and we would watch the dailies, the film that had been shot the day before.

There were continual script adjustments to be made as problems arose, and I kept making them as quickly as they were called for.

Finally, a three-hour rough cut of the film was assembled and we all gathered in a screening room in Robert Stigwood's Beverly Hills mansion to watch the result. Three hours later, I knew the vision I had had in my mind was not the vision I had seen on the screen. I could feel the disappointment of the other people in the room.

There was an uneasy silence and all eyes were focused on the producer.

Robert was defiant. "I love this movie," he declared, "and I'm going to give it the biggest premiere in the history of Hollywood. Then I'm going to fly everyone to New York and stage the biggest premiere in New York's history. Then we'll see what the world has to say about our lovely, lovely, film."

Five hundred thousand dollars was to be allotted to stage the two opening nights. The film would open in

Los Angeles at the Cinerama Dome Theatre on July 21, 1978. It would be followed by a lavish ball at the Century Plaza Hotel in Beverly Hills. Two days after that, Stigwood, the Bee Gees, George Burns, Alice Cooper, Earth, Wind and Fire, and key members of the film staff, as well as the reporters assigned to cover the event, would board a chartered plane to fly to New York for the East Coast premiere.

In a burst of creativity, Robert's publicity managers had agreed to have the plane land at Kennedy Airport in time to have its arrival carried live by CBS and NBC. The television crews would be stationed on a cordoned-off airstrip in the freight delivery section of the airport. The next day, officially designated as "Sgt. Pepper's Lonely Hearts Club Band Day," would find all the principals at a well-publicized morning ceremony at City Hall to hear an official proclamation read in their honor by Mayor Koch.

The New York premiere was to be a hundred-dollar-a-ticket performance at the Radio City Music Hall for the benefit of the Police Athletic League. The performance would be followed by a midnight supper at Roseland and a dancing party at Studio 54, which was to start at 2 A.M. and go on till dawn.

Esther had told me about her dream of attending an opening night of mine. Would there ever be a bigger opening than this? I wanted Esther and Sam to be with me that night in New York. I hoped Esther would feel that she was up to it.

I carefully outlined the entire event to her over the phone. I could sense that the invitation made her nervous.

"I have nothing to wear."

"As your birthday present, I'll give you the money to buy a really pretty dress," I said. "I'll send a limousine to the apartment to pick you up. You'll come into New York and do the town."

"Tell Sam about it." Esther sounded too nervous to continue the discussion.

Once again I described the evening.

"I'd like to go," Sam said enthusiastically. "It sounds terrific to me."

Esther got back on the phone. "What do you think?" I asked.

"I don't know," she replied. "I really want to go and I feel better than I've felt in a long time, but I don't know if I'm brave enough to stand the noise and the crowds."

"I'm going to buy the tickets now anyway."

"What happens if I don't go? Will you be able to sell them?"

"Don't worry about it."

"I'll let you know."

Esther, Sam and Mrs. Gordy sat having coffee.

"I'm going to pray real hard for you so that you'll be able to go to that opening," Mrs. Gordy said as she stirred the sugar into her coffee.

"I don't think I can do it."

"Why?" asked Sam.

"I am getting better. I know that. But somehow I'm just not right and I may never be totally right, and all I think about is that it could happen again."

Esther got up and went into the bedroom and lay down, but she could not sleep. Suddenly, she sat up. She wanted to go to the premiere. Sam wanted her to go; Henry wanted her to go. So what if she was tired and felt self-conscious. It didn't bother them; why then should it bother her? She wondered if she could pull herself up by her bootstraps and make herself go.

She got out of bed and walked back into the living room. Sam was reading the newspaper.

"Hi," she said.

"Hi," Sam replied, looking up.

"I want to go to the premiere."

Sam broke into a smile. Mrs. Gordy did too. "That's wonderful," Sam said.

"But I'm afraid."

"What are you afraid of?"

"I've got to pull myself up by my bootstraps. I know that. But there's a million little things I'm afraid of."

"Do you want to make a list?"

"Yes," said Esther. "I want to make a list of everything I'm afraid of and all the problems I might have, and then I want to solve each and every one of them."

"Let's do it," said Sam.

They sat at the dining room table. Sam took out a legal pad and a ballpoint pen.

Esther began to speak. "I'm afraid I might not be able to get up in the morning; I'm afraid to go out at night; I'm afraid I might fall asleep at the party and not be able to stay up that late; I'm afraid other people might stare at me because I still move stiffly; I'm afraid I might not have anything to say. . . ."

"Is that it?"

"I also need a new dress and I have to go to the beauty parlor. It's going to be very expensive."

"But that's not what's bothering you. Is there anything more that's bothering you?"

"Isn't that list long enough?"

Sam and Esther studied the list. Together, they worked out a battle plan. Every day for a week Esther would get up at eight-thirty in the morning. She would stay out of bed the whole day. If she got very tired, she would be allowed to take a nap in the afternoon, for only an hour. In addition, she would try to stay up to watch the eleven o'clock news every other night and then try to watch the beginning of Johnny Carson, whom she'd always enjoyed but had not been able to stay up for since her hospitalization. Sam and she would begin to go out more in the evenings. On Saturday they would try to go to a movie, a play, a restaurant—it didn't matter what, so long as Esther would learn not to feel self-conscious in public. Although friends had been dropping in, they would invite one or two couples to visit them for Sunday brunch. When Esther felt more at ease, they would give a small dinner party.

"If I survive seven eight-thirty mornings, three midnight nights, four Saturday nights outs, four Sunday brunches and one dinner party, I can survive anything," said Esther.

"Do you want to start tomorrow morning?"

"Slave driver!" Esther exclaimed. "If we're going to go to Studio 54, we'll also have to take disco lessons."

"Do you want to start tomorrow morning?" Sam asked again.

"Yes," said Esther. "Yes. Yes. Yes. We'll begin tomorrow morning."

Esther then called me to say that she was going to try to go. She described her new schedule.

It was March; she had four and a half months in which to practice.

33. The alarm went off at seven-thirty. Esther rolled over and sat up. She was amazed that she was awake. She leaned over and shook Sam.

"What's the matter?" he asked.

"It's seven-thirty. What are you still doing in bed? Up and at 'em, Sammy-o, up and at 'em."

Esther climbed slowly out of bed. She wobbled out of the bedroom and into the kitchen. She put the kettle up.

"What do you want for breakfast?" she called to Sam.

Sam stood outside the kitchen, staring. "Are you sure you don't need any help?" he asked.

"I'm sure. Tell me what you'd like for breakfast."

"Orange juice, a bagel and coffee."

"That's not very nutritious," said Esther.

"What should I have? Eggs?"

"Eggs aren't very good for you. They've got cholesterol."

"Then what should I have?"

"Why do you think I've stayed in bed?" said Esther. "Look at all the questions I've spared myself."

Esther made breakfast—orange juice, scrambled eggs, toasted bagels and coffee. It was the first breakfast she had made in twenty months. They sat down and ate it. They were finished at eight-fifteen. Esther showered, got dressed and made up her face.

"I'm going to get the paper," said Sam.

"I'll go with you." Esther took his arm. Together, they strolled through the little Long Island village, with its old trees and pleasant streets, and did some early-morning shopping.

When Mrs. Gordy arrived, she was astonished to see Esther up and about. "What are you doing, Mrs. Katz?" she asked.

"I'm practicing being normal," Esther replied.

"But how do you feel?"

"I've got to pull myself up from the bootstraps. And it hurts and I'm tired, but I'm not going to stop."

Esther insisted on making Mrs. Gordy breakfast. Then they went out for their walk.

Sam watched them go. He hoped Esther could keep it up.

Esther's determination to go to the opening night gave her the strength to stick to the tough schedule that she had imposed on herself. The first night she stayed up till one minute past twelve; she was up again at eight-thirty the next morning and stayed up that night till the same late hour.

Now she had a fifteen-and-a-half-hour day to fill and as she searched for things to do, her curiosity began to return. Interests that had lain dormant came back to life as her concentration improved. She resumed going to flea markets and antique fairs. She could listen to music and wanted to go to the movies. She started cooking. She began to read again, devouring two and three new novels a week. The more interest she took in things, the more energy she had. The more energetic she became, the more she resembled her old self.

In the mornings, Mrs. Gordy and she would stroll through the village, window-shopping for an outfit to wear at the premiere. Occasionally they would go into a store and Esther would try something on. Esther would always proudly explain that she was looking for something to wear to her son's opening night.

As time passed she became more excited. About a month after Esther had begun her "bootstrap" and Studio 54 routine, she and Sam joined a local beach club. They quickly made friends with many of the members. Soon they had joined a group that went out every Saturday night, usually to a concert. Before the concert they all went to dinner and after it they went to the home of one of the members of the group for coffee and cake. After the third Saturday evening, Sam was surprised to hear Esther announce that next week it was Sam's and her turn to have the gang at her house.

At the end of three months, they went over their checklist. Esther could now get up every morning; she could stay up late without falling asleep if she wanted to; she could mingle unselfconsciously with people and easily make small talk. They had done everything on their list but give the dinner party.

"Let's go for broke," said Esther, having decided she would give the biggest party she had ever given. She called all their old friends and all their new ones and invited them to a belated housewarming.

It was decided that Esther should enjoy the party so they had it catered. Esther would cook at the next one. There were beautiful platters of cold cuts as well as hors d'oeuvres and delicious desserts. Mrs. Gordy helped serve the food and a young unemployed actor— the son of one of the guests—acted as bartender.

Her old friends—many of whom had visited her at Chelsea and had thought then that she might never get better—were amazed at the good shape she was in. Her new friends could not believe that she had been hospitalized twice for mental illness.

Everyone had a wonderful time. At the height of the festivities, they all sang "For they're a jolly good couple" to Esther and Sam.

"Thank you," Esther replied. "Both to those of you who knew me when I was off my rocker, and those of you who met me when I got back on. All I can say is now I'm not going to fall off anymore."

Because the opening was to take place in the summer and the weather would be hot, Esther had taken my birthday money and had selected a long, soft plaid silk skirt. On top she would wear a white ruffled blouse made of a material that she later described as silk organza. Sam also insisted that she buy new shoes and a new evening bag. She had not wanted to spend the extra money, but Sam said that he wanted his best girl to look wonderful.

After they had picked up all the clothes, Esther modeled them for Sam and Mrs. Gordy, who began oohing and aahing the minute Esther stepped from the bedroom.

"Do you think I'll be discovered on opening night?" Esther said jestingly. "Maybe *I'll* be the next member of this family to go to Hollywood."

"Now you're ready to come to church with me," said Mrs. Gordy. "You'll come to the service and stay for a real Southern dinner."

"Whenever you invite me," said Esther, "I'll be there."

Three Sundays later, Esther and Sam set out for the Star of Zion Baptist Church.

Mrs. Gordy was waiting for them at the church door. She embraced Esther excitedly and escorted them inside. Sam and Esther could feel the eyes of the congregation on them as Mrs. Gordy led them to the front of the church and placed them in the first row, directly opposite the pulpit. On each chair was a small red prayer book, a fan and a program, so that they could follow the service.

At eleven sharp, Dr. Smith, dressed in black ministerial robes, took his place in the pulpit. He smiled down at Esther and Sam. The choir appeared in the back of the church. All women, they were attired in long light-blue robes. "We can't get a man who wants to sing," Mrs. Gordy whispered as the women came down the aisle, singing a rousing "We've Come This Far by Faith."

"Glory be," one woman called out.

"Amen," shouted another.

"Every congregation has a few screamers," Mrs. Gordy explained.

In a mellifluous yet powerful voice, Dr. Smith began the service with a few remarks of welcome. There was a brief meditation. The choir then sang a hymn of welcome, "Now Thank You, Lord, We Are One."

Esther loved the singing. It was full of energy and enthusiasm, qualities she had come to value greatly. Dr. Smith led the congregation in prayer and the prayers were followed by more singing. The minister then addressed himself to the visitors.

"When our beloved Minna Gordy, had some hard times, our visitors in the first row, Mr. and Mrs. Katz, helped her. Mrs. Gordy came originally to help them and the Lord saw fit to move them to help her in return. Now Mrs. Gordy has a good apartment near our church that she can afford. Any friends of Mrs. Gordy's are friends of ours. We welcome you to the Star of Zion Baptist Church. We've all been praying for you. Having you here is proof that our prayers have been answered."

A choir member stepped forward to sing a solo. There was another prayer.

Dr. Smith then urged everyone to contribute to the burial fund. Esther looked puzzled, and Mrs. Gordy whispered, "All of us believe in a proper burial. But it's getting more and more expensive to bury a person. So we have a fund to help anyone who can't foot the bill."

Everyone began to sing. Row by row, starting with the first, the congregation marched to the front of the church to place contributions in a box. When everyone had had his turn, the entire congregation rose to sing a rousing gospel song.

Dr. Smith read from the Scriptures. The reading was the basis of his sermon, "Retaliation, Love and Hatred."

For almost forty-five minutes he spoke of the hideous consequences of violence and revenge. He urged everyone to develop the spiritual strength to avoid both. "Two minutes of love will do more than all the violence and revenge in the world."

Everyone stood and joined hands in a circle of prayer. Esther prayed for Sam and Mrs. Gordy and she felt Sam and Mrs. Gordy were praying for her. She felt the power of everyone in the church focused on trying to do something good.

The service was over and the choir began to sing for the last time.

"How are you feeling?" Mrs. Gordy asked Esther.

"Wonderful."

After the service everyone adjourned to the basement community room for dinner. Each month a different member of the congregation did the cooking. It was a real feast.

After dinner, Dr. Smith asked to speak privately with Esther and Sam. They went into the backyard behind the church. Dr. Smith thanked them for coming. "I have to ask you a favor," he said.

"What can we do?" asked Esther.

"I got a call from Mrs. Gordy's doctor this week—"

"What's the matter?" Esther interrupted.

"Her heart is not in good shape . . ." said Dr. Smith. Esther began to cry.

"What can we do?" asked Sam.

"She still gets up early each morning to come to you, when she should be home resting. She's too ill to work anymore. It's time she retired once and for all. We will look after her and make sure she wants for nothing. She's given so much of her energy to our church; we in turn would like to give some of our energy to her."

"She really should not exert herself," said Esther. "I agree with you—she must retire."

"But she's too proud to tell you that she's too frail to work anymore, and besides, she loves you too much to leave you. You must tell her that you are strong enough to go it on your own and thank her for a job well done. She'll still have her pride and you'll be saving her life."

"You are a very nice man, Dr. Smith," said Sam.

They stepped inside.

"What did Dr. Smith want?" asked Mrs. Gordy, who couldn't imagine what they had been talking about.

"He wanted to tell me what a lovely lady you are," said Esther.

Mrs. Gordy smiled proudly.

"He also wanted to tell me what a lovely lady I am," Esther added.

"You are, you are," said Mrs. Gordy.

Esther knew that she would miss her terribly.

That night Esther rehearsed in her mind what she was going to say to Mrs. Gordy. She kept changing things around and there was a part of her that felt she wasn't ready to go it entirely on her own. But she kept reminding herself that Mrs. Gordy had to go. Finally, she was satisfied.

The next day she delivered her carefully prepared speech. "I have something very sad to tell you," she said to Mrs. Gordy. "Something that I've been trying to tell you for a week. Something that distresses me very much."

"What it it?" asked Mrs. Gordy.

"I went to see Dr. Sudhalter last week and he told me that I am still too dependent on you," Esther blurted out. "He said I won't totally recover until I do everything on my own. He said that I have to let you go."

Mrs. Gordy stared at Esther.

"I told him I wouldn't consider it."

"You have to!" Mrs. Gordy exclaimed. "It's for your own good."

"I can't!"

Mrs. Gordy said nothing and Esther sensed she was searching for the right thing to say. But Esther could see that Mrs. Gordy was trying to hide her relief. "I think you're doing the right thing, Mrs. Katz," she finally said. "You are well enough to be on your own, and you should be. But if you ever need me, you know that I'll hurry right back."

"I'm going to miss you," said Esther, "miss you terribly."

"I'm going to miss you too."

There was a moment of silence.

"What are you going to do now?" Esther asked.

"I'm finally going to be a retired lady and take a long rest."

"Sam and I will come and pick you up and we'll all go out together. We're going to be friends now. And if *you* ever need *me,* you let me know and I will hurry to you."

They decided to turn their leavetaking into a celebration, so Esther made Sam take them out for hot fudge sundaes. They drove Mrs. Gordy to the train station and Esther and Sam walked her to the platform.

The train was pulling in. They kissed each other goodbye and Mrs. Gordy got on the train.

"She'll fool them all," Esther said as the train pulled away. "She's a fighter. She's going to live a long time." She looked in Sam's eyes. "Well, Sam," she said with a smile, "it looks like it's just you and me from now on."

34. Three weeks before I was to return to New York for the *Sgt. Pepper* opening, Esther called to report that she was at the end of her second month with no symptoms at all. When she had visited Dr. Sudhalter, he was impressed by the progress she had made. "He's begun to reduce my medication," she told me. "I can't wait to see you and show you how well I'm doing."

"I'll be there before you know it," I replied. "How would you like to come to the airport and watch the plane land?"

Esther laughed. "That may be too hectic even for me."

We talked some more and then we hung up.

The lilt in her voice was back; there was no doubt about that. It was a sound I had been afraid I would never hear again.

The Los Angeles premiere of *Sgt. Pepper* had gone off splendidly. After a day of rest, the *Sgt. Pepper* cast and staff were whisked to the freight entrance of Los Angeles International Airport, where a chartered plane was waiting to take us to New York.

In New York, the preparations for the arrival of the *Sgt. Pepper* plane had already begun. Checkpoints had been set up throughout the airport to keep Bee Gees fans away from the freight area where the plane would land. Security guards, keeping in touch with each other by walkie-talkie, roamed the terminal, making sure only invited members of the press, the city government and the Police Athletic League, all wearing the proper Security buttons, got onto the airstrip.

Esther was puttering around in the kitchen, when she suddenly turned off all the gas jets. "I want to see Henry as soon as he comes in," she announced. "Let's go to the airport."

Sam stared at her. "He told us it's going to be a mad-house."

"But our names are on the guest list. I'm going to comb my hair and put on some lipstick."

He looked at her. She was really excited. "Okay. Let's go."

After parking their car at the airport, they headed for the airstrip. Sam spotted the barricade first. Three guards patrolled the gate.

"Leave it to me," said Esther.

"Where's your Security button?" the guard asked as Sam and Esther approached him.

"I don't have a Security button," Esther replied, "but there wouldn't be a movie without me. I gave birth to the author."

The guard looked at them. If these were two senior-citizen Bee Gees freaks and this was their scam, they deserved to get onto the landing strip. "Come in," he said.

Esther and Sam marched out onto the runway. Fifty members of the Police Athletic League Drum and Bugle Corps were poised to play; twenty other PAL members were carrying bouquets of flowers for the celebrities. Francis Plimpton, the official New York City greeter, was there carrying the key to the city to present to Robert Stigwood. The NBC and CBS television news crews, as well as fifty reporters assigned to the event, huddled together waiting for the plane. Hundreds of others milled around and no one knew exactly who they were or what they were doing there. But everyone was having a good time.

Esther and Sam made their way to the front of the crowd. People stood looking upward, in expectation of the *Sgt. Pepper* plane's appearance in the sky.

The plane landed and we were waiting for the staircase to be rolled up so that we could disembark. Robert roamed the plane, talking to several of the passengers. As he got to my seat, he happened to look out the window. "There's the man who's going to give me the key to the city," he told me.

"Where?"

I followed the direction of his arm and spotted Mr. Duke in the midst of the enormous crowd.

"My God!" I said. "Those are my parents standing next to him."

There were spotlights focused on the exits so the television cameras could get a clear picture of the stars as they descended from the plane. I pushed my way through the crowd and threw my arms around Esther and Sam.

The noise, the music, the cameras, the lights, the flowers, the screaming crowd—it was an enormously exciting party. At that moment, it seemed as if it was just for us.

Robert had arranged for all the *Pepper* people to stay at the Hotel Plaza. The giant, smooth-running Stigwood machine was hastening us there, where interviews had been scheduled until midnight. I barely had time to remind Esther and Sam that they were to meet me at the hotel the following afternoon.

The next day, the limousine brought them to the Plaza. Esther looked radiant in her new outfit. Her skin had recovered its former gleam and smoothness, and her eyes sparkled. We had drinks and then it was time to leave for the premiere. Twenty thousand fans crowded the route to Radio City Music Hall and we proceeded slowly through the mob, the police having to clear our way.

After the film, we were driven to Roseland for the supper party. The entire room had been transformed into a replica of Heartland and everything looked wonderful. The food was delicious, the music was lovely, and the champagne flowed. Everybody was in terrific spirits and Esther and Sam had a chance to meet George Burns, one of their all-time favorites, and to have their picture taken with Alice Cooper. Esther told Alice that she had always admired the way he dressed.

The reviews of the film were already in the newspapers and someone slipped them to me. They were uniformly terrible. If this had been a movie, instead of real life, I reflected, the reviews would have been raves. Nevertheless, as I watched Esther and Sam enjoying every moment of the party, I realized that nothing could diminish the magic of this night.

At Studio 54, Sam danced with Dianne Steinberg, the beautiful young woman who played Lucy in the movie, and I danced with Esther. At four in the morning, Sam and Esther climbed into the limousine and were driven home.

It took me until late the next day to recuperate from the event. In the afternoon I took the train to Long Island.

"We're still euphoric," Esther announced when she saw me. "It was one of the happiest nights of my life." She went back into the kitchen to finish making dinner.

"How am I doing?" Esther asked as she set the table.

"Even better than you told me you were," I replied, meaning every word of it.

"Thank you. Two years ago, I lost all control of myself. Then my control was determined only by the amount and kind of medication I took. Now, slowly, my control has come back. It makes me appreciate every single thing I do. Now, believe it or not, when I set the table I appreciate the fact that I can do it, because a year ago I wanted to and couldn't." Esther put down the last fork, turned, and gave me a big hug.

Sam asked me if I would walk him to the bakery to pick up a special cake they had ordered for dinner. On the way, he told me over and over how pleased he was by Esther's progress. "Ordinary, little things that you never think about—things that once bored me—have become special to me. I see a significance in little things that I never saw before.

"We all walk on thin ice every day of our lives," he continued as we left the bakery. "If we thought about it, we'd all go nuts. And then one day, when you least expect it, you fall through the ice. Esther fell through it. We grabbed on to her. But we went too. The point is that you can't always climb out—but we did. We all helped each other to climb out, and I'm going to be grateful for that for the rest of my life."

When we got back to the apartment, we took our places at the table. As I sat there, Sam's words kept running through my mind. The food, the conversation, the atmosphere—all of it was extremely pleasant—and thoroughly normal. It was the first normal meal the three of us had had together in almost two years.

I looked at my father: he was right. It wasn't just normal; it was wondrous. I was as grateful as he was.

Acknowledgments

I wish to thank my mother's current psychiatrist, Arthur K. Shapiro, M.D., who read the sections of this book dealing with psychiatric medication to make sure they were accurate; my internist Michael Gitter, M.D., who checked all of the other medical information; and Robert N. Butler, M.D., Director of the National Institute on Aging, who freely gave of his time to discuss with me the problems of aging and mental illness in America.

My thanks also to Ron Bernstein who fought tirelessly for this book from the day he read the first page; Caroline Shookhoff, whose good humor and intelligence helped make the writing of this book a pleasure; Barbara J. Harris, Geoffrey Sanford, Felice Willat, and Myrna Zimmerman were always there when I needed them; and, especially, my editor Cynthia Merman, without whom this book would not have been possible.

During the writing of this book I was the recipient of the support and unstinting generosity of Rod Steiger. The world knows Mr. Steiger as an artist of the first magnitude; I am privileged to know him as a compassionate human being.

Renée Sacks devoted many hours of her time to reading and improving this manuscript. This book reflects her intelligence as well as her devotion. I am proud to be her friend.

Finally, I must thank Dr. Eugene E. Landy. Dr. Landy cared deeply enough about me to teach me how to quiet my inner noises so that I could say and do what I really wanted to. Without him I could never have been free. I will always be grateful.